WHAT WAS HOT: 1969

THE MOVIES

Easy Rider, with Peter Fonda, Dennis Hopper and a very young Jack Nicholson.

Midnight Cowboy, with Dustin Hoffman and Jon Voight. It is the first X-rated film to win an Oscar.

Butch Cassidy and the Sundance Kid, with Paul Newman and Robert Redford.

MUSIC

"Tommy," by The Who.

"Abbey Road," by The Beatles.

"A Boy Named Sue," by Johnny Cash.

"Leaving on a Jet Plane," by Peter, Paul and Mary.

IN THE NEWS

Neil Armstrong is the first human to walk on the moon.

Senator Edward M. Kennedy is involved in the accident at Chappaquidick.

The Manson family slaughters Sharon Tate and others in her Los Angeles household.

The Woodstock Music Festival.

SPORTS

The Amazing New York Mets win the World Series.

The New York Jets led by a cocky quarterback Joe Namath beat the Baltimore Colts.

FADS

America discovers the water bed.

What Was Hot!

a rollercoaster ride
through six decades of
pop culture in america

Julian Biddle

CITADEL PRESS
Kensington Publishing Corp.
www.kensingtonbooks.com

CITADEL PRESS BOOKS are published by

Kensington Publishing Corp.
850 Third Avenue
New York, NY 10022

All Kensington titles, imprints, and distributed lines are available at special quantity discounts for bulk purchases for sales promotions, premiums, fund-raising, educational, or institutional use. Special book excerpts or customized printings can also be created to fit specific needs. For details, write or phone the office of the Kensington special sales manager: Kensington Publishing Corp., 850 Third Avenue, New York, NY 10022, attn: Special Sales Department, phone 1-800-221-2647.

Citadel Press and the Citadel Logo are trademarks of Kensington Publishing Corp.

First Citadel printing: November 2001

10 9 8 7 6 5 4 3 2

Printed in the United States of America

Library of Congress Control Number: 2001092403

ISBN 0-8065-2311-5

With gratitude to my mother
and to the memory of my father.

CONTENTS

Foreword

We Americans define ourselves by the things we choose to do, by the music we listen to, by the movies we buy tickets for, by the larger-than-life celebrities we follow in magazines. We're also a country of sports enthusiasts, spending millions of dollars a year on athletic events. Can you imagine *America* without *baseball?*

These elements form our unique national character. In many ways, America leads the world in shaping popular culture. Some of our biggest exporters are our entertainment industries. Everyone knows Michael Jackson and Sylvester Stallone. The world over, Madonna can be identified by young and old.

America's dominance of the world's pop culture is nothing new. After all, there were very few people on the planet who did not know Elvis Presley at the height of his fame. Apparently some people still recognize him in their midst.

It was television more than any one other device that changed how we saw ourselves. We were peaking into each other's homes, seeing how the Ricardos lived, seeing how much better off the Nortons were than the Kramdens. Mothers dressed one way on television and differently in real life. But television mothers were the ideal. Television fathers acted one way on the tube, but far differently in real life. Some say all this confusion led a great number of people to therapy.

Television also changed how the world viewed us because we sent our situation comedies and medical dramas and westerns around the world. Some foreigners might have been shocked to learn that the average American woman did not act and dress like Alexis Carrington and that the average American boy did not have his own family band like with Keith Partridge.

Pop culture tells us who we are at any given moment in time.

That's why "The Donna Reed Show" once immensely popular, looks more than dated in its situations; it looks embarrassingly naive. But maybe the country was naive. Could a situation comedy after the arrival of The Beatles get away with an episode about the length of a teenage boy's hair? "All in the Family" seems strident and more abrasive than funny today. But it was aired during strident and abrasive times.

Times change so quickly, it is nearly impossible to keep track of what was popular only a year ago. Hopefully this year by year chronology will spark the flame of memory—"Oh, I remember that song. I was in high school at that time." It might also lead to discussion of a certain time period, a certain subject matter.

Ask any ten people what was hot in any given year, and you are sure to get ten completely different answers. It is literally impossible to have listed all the things of importance in any given year. This is not meant to be an almanac. It is the story of pop culture in America.

When a choice had to be made of one item to include over others, the choice was always made in favor of the most emblematic of the selections. Therefore, some people might not find their favorite, say "Burke's Law" or *Nightmare on Elm Street,* among these pages. There is likely to be some disagreement over omissions, but they might not have been hot enough.

This is meant to be a fun and informative ride through recent popular culture. Enjoy the scenery.

                                                      J. B.

Acknowledgments

The author would like to thank the following people for their help: Joe Rosado, Fred Westbrook, Arlene Crowe, Suzanne E. Stone, David Hajdu, Jean Ryburn, Ewa Maraszkiewicz, Beth Schoch, and Jonathan Cohen; the good people of Fort Greene, Patricia Jempty, Marty Feigen, and Fred Johnson; Donald and Ronni Moore; the sales force at Pinnacle, Lynn Brown, Enza Lozito, Eileen Bertelli, and Bill Hogan (extra thanks, Bill); the staff of Seton Hall University Library, especially Anthony Lee; editor Paul Dinas, Elise Donner, and last but by no means least John Scognamiglio.

THE
1950s

The children of returning World War II veterans were a new breed of Americans. Their experiences and influences were like no other generation before them. The nation had come out of the war stronger and more powerful and more affluent than ever before America was the proud, rich godfather of the world. American parents were willing and very able to share this affluence with their children, having themselves been deprived of so much during the Depression of the 1930s.

The veterans were purchasing affordable tract housing in what was a new cultural phenomenon, the suburbs. Their children were part of a new America where everyone was finally equal, or at least it seemed that way, because everyone was living in houses that looked so much alike.

The greatest equalizer throughout the country was that other new acquisition, the big and clunky machine that sat in the middle of the living room, the thing that was destined to monopolize the time and thinking of generations of young Americans: the television. These new Americans, later called Baby Boomers, were the first Television Generation. But not only was the television a source of information and entertainment, it became both friend and baby-sitter. America, and especially America's children, were now tuned in, and they tuned in every day.

The power and influence of television changed the way America lived, changed the way it did business, and how it thought. The communication of ideas was now instantaneous. Products were now being sold via commercials aimed at the young. The young, being susceptible to new ideas, "needed" the things they now saw advertised on television. If it was on television, after all, it had to be good, and it had to be owned.

It was not only the products the public craved however. There were stars who came right into people's homes. Certainly Lucille

Ball and Jackie Gleason were stars before they came to the small screen, but it was in our living rooms that their special talents exploded and took hold and kept us enthralled. Television made stars of so many people, virtually overnight, it is impossible to think of what our cultural heritage would be like without them. Who is the most famous sewer worker in America, then or now? It must be Art Carney's Ed Norton. And William Frawley's Fred Mertz is the definition of curmudgeon.

Movie stars were thought of as traitors if they defected to the burgeoning industry of the small screen. Some were threatened that their movie careers would be over or at least tarnished beyond repair if they accepted the often-lucrative television series. Some stars, seeing that their career in films had run its course, gladly signed to star on a weekly basis. Some, such as the glamorous Loretta Young, became even bigger stars on the small screen and are most remembered for their work there.

The Hollywood movie industry mistrusted and feared television. Producers and film executives worried that audiences would stay home and watch free television instead of paying to see a movie at the local theatre. Their fears were justified. Television audiences were extremely loyal to their viewing habits. Who needed to go and see a comedy at the Rialto when Uncle Miltie was on the TV?

Hollywood had to come up with a few good ideas to convince moviegoers to keep lining up at the movies. After all, going to the movies was as American as apple pie. America had invented the movies. Audiences had always been loyal. Something had to be done to get them back into the theatres. Movies became bigger and filled with color. More provocative themes came to the screen, as did films with a social conscience. The new, wider screen was filled with performers who were a whole new breed of actor. The era of the taciturn leading man was fading into the sunset. The dark and brooding stars, such as Montgomery Clift and James Dean, were taking over. Seemingly overnight, movies were alive again with a new vigor. In the early years of the fifties one man embodied the excitement of going to the movies. He was Marlon Brando.

It took the music industry a little longer to catch the wave. If

America had been quietly listening to standards by such great and respected composers as Irving Berlin and Jerome Kern sung by such melodious singers as Bing Crosby and Rosemary Clooney, things were about to get loud and raucous. One of the great forces of nature appeared on the music scene and changed everything, both musically and by extension culturally, forever. There was no way a poor boy from Tupelo, Mississippi, could have known that his career dreams would succeed to such an extent as to alter the way people lived. That force of nature was Elvis Presley.

The old guard was changing elsewhere as well, although it certainly was not fading away. The glory that was the New York Yankees did not diminish when the "Yankee Clipper" Joe DiMaggio, a true American hero, retired. The era of Mickey Mantle and the pennant-winning boys in pinstripes captured the hearts and minds and imaginations of sports fans, especially young boys, from all forty-eight states. Baseball was everywhere, even on television.

Beneath the smiling surface of the 1950s were darker matters, much left untouched. In the Deep South, racial tensions grew out of the long-established standard operating procedures, which were grossly unfair to the Negroes, as African-Americans were called. Bitterness and resentment were seeds planted deeply in the fields and towns and villages of Alabama, Mississippi, and other Southern states unwilling to accept the Declaration of Independence which said "all men are created equal."

An underground movement of writers, headed by such people as Allen Ginsberg and Jack Kerouac, were called The Beats. Made up of disaffected poets and college intellectuals, this loose-knit group met in coffeehouses and on campuses, spoke and wrote about youthful alienation and the aimlessness of society. They and their followers were called Beatniks; they brought about the bongo-drum craze, used as accompaniment to their dramatic poetry.

In November 1952, General Dwight D. Eisenhower, the hero of World War II, was elected president of the United States by his fellow countrymen, many of whom had served in the military. It was only right and fitting that one of the true heroes and winners of the 1940s should again ascend to power in the following decade, suc-

ceeding "Give 'em Hell" Harry S. Truman. President Ike Eisenhower made sense. He had been a leader before; he was grand-
fatherly and seemed kind, no matter how battle-weary. He knew the
enemy. He was the ideal captain of the ship of state as the United
States sailed the waters of the 1950s. With his big, reassuring grin,
no one could dispute that everything was fine, everything was safe,
everything was going to get better. With the World War and the
Korean Conflict behind us, the 50's held no chance of failure in
America's future.

1950

THE MOVIES

All About Eve directed by Joseph L. Mankiewicz. Bette Davis delivered venomous one-liners as the incomparable Margo Channing, a major Broadway diva. Top-notch cast included Anne Baxter, Celeste Holm, George Sanders, Thelma Ritter, and a very young Marilyn Monroe. *Eve* captured Best Picture Oscar, and Sanders won Best Supporting Actor for his cynical performance.

Sunset Boulevard directed by Billy Wilder. Gloria Swanson was unforgettable as faded movie queen Norma Desmond. William Holden played hack writer Joe Gillis. Nancy Olson contributed a memorable performance, and Erich von Stroheim embodied the noble ex-husband Max. Real-life faded stars showed up in bit parts: Buster Keaton, Anna Q. Nilsson, and H. B. Warner.

Father of the Bride directed by Vincente Minnelli. Spencer Tracy played the title character to Elizabeth Taylor's young wife-to-be. Joan Bennett costarred as the ever-loving wife. The mores of the 1950s were demonstrated here: rich father, glamorous daughter, and the wedding as the most significant cultural focus.

Samson and Delilah directed by Cecil B. DeMille. Grand and sweeping and totally camp. Victor Mature and Hedy Lamarr were the title players, one more ravishing than the other. Spectacles like this one packed in audiences.

Cinderella, the Disney classic. Evil stepsisters have always made for a good story.

THE PLAYERS

Macho-yet-handicapped Marlon Brando starred in *The Men.*

Prissy-but-lovable Clifton Webb starred in *Cheaper by the Dozen.*

Come-back movie queen Gloria Swanson was Norma Desmond in *Sunset Boulevard.*

MUSIC

"The Tennessee Waltz" by Patti Page, the singing rage.

"Goodnight, Irene" by The Weavers with Gordon Jenkins and his orchestra.

"The Third Man Theme" by Anton Karas.

LITERATURE

Ernest Hemingway's *Across the River and into the Trees* was published.

IN THE NEWS

General Douglas MacArthur was appointed commander of United Nations Forces in Korea.

SPORTS

Arthur Larsen won United States Lawn Tennis championship.

The New York Yankees beat the Philadelphia Phillies four-zip in the World Series.

In golf, the U.S. Open was won by Ben Hogan.

TELEVISION

"Your Show of Shows" featured Sid Caesar and Imogene Coca.

"Texaco Star Theater" starred "Mr. Television" Milton Berle.

Also Notable: The arrival of "The George Burns and Gracie Allen Show"; "What's My Line?" with Arlene Francis and Dorothy Kilgallen; "The Jack Benny Program."

On September 4, 1950, Jean Muir, one of the stars of the popular show "The Aldrich Family," was dropped by the sponsor General Foods. Although not a Communist or a sympathizer, Muir was fired. This was just one of the many "witchhunts" of the era brought about by Senator Joseph McCarthy's fanatical desire to rid America of "Reds."

1951

THE MOVIES

A Streetcar Named Desire directed by Elia Kazan. Tennessee Williams adapted his own hit Broadway play for the screen. Marlon Brando bellowed as the brutish Stanley Kowalski, making torn T-shirts famous; Vivien Leigh played yet another Southern belle; Kim Hunter and Karl Malden excelled in supporting roles. These three walked away with Oscars; Brando lost to the sympathy-nostalgic vote for Bogart. The language and subject matter were tough, and the magic of movie making would never be the same after this tour-de-force.

The African Queen directed by John Huston. Ocsar-winner Humphrey Bogart played the gin-swizzled Charlie Alnutt opposite the prim and very proper Katharine Hepburn, doing a wonderful Eleanor Roosevelt imitation. The locations really were shot in Africa, and the Congo never seemed so much fun. This was one of the first major Hollywood productions to venture so far out of the studio.

A Place in the Sun directed by George Stevens. Poor boy Montgomery Cliff set his sights on glam-girl Elizabeth Taylor while having a similarly poor and plain girl Shelley Winters pregnant with his child. Class struggle was never so beautifully photographed. America ate it up.

THE PLAYERS

Uncomplicated John Wayne soared in *The Flying Leathernecks.*

Very complicated Montgomery Clift emoted in *A Place in the Sun.*

The blonde queen of Twentieth Century Fox, Betty Grable, sashayed in *Call Me Mister.*

MUSIC

"Cry" by Johnnie Ray.

"Because of You" by Tony Bennett.

"How High the Moon" by married guitarists Les Paul and Mary Ford.

LITERATURE

Perennial college-prep read *Catcher in the Rye* by reclusive J. D. Salinger debuted. Disenfranchised Holden Caulfield served generation after generation of young Americans as a role model.

The Caine Mutiny by Herman Wouk told the story of unbalanced Captain Queeg whose command was overturned during World War II.

IN THE NEWS

On April 11, President Harry S. Truman dismissed General Douglas MacArthur after they disagreed about the larger spread of the Korean War throughout Southeast Asia.

SPORTS

"Jersey" Joe Walcott knocked off Ezzard Charles to win heavyweight championship title.

Race horse Citation's earnings reached over $1 million with the win of Hollywood Gold Cup.

Australia won Davis Cup against U.S.

TELEVISION

Homespun Arthur Godfrey starred in his "Talent Scouts."

"I Love Lucy" entered the picture. "Queen of the B Movies," Lucille Ball and her husband, bandleader Desi Arnaz, revolutionized television with their three-camera setup. That was all technical; on a talent level, they were unsurpassable. The adventures of Lucy and Ricky and their pals the Mertzes (Vivian Vance and William Frawley) became enduring American symbols, something like Lady Liberty.

1952

THE MOVIES

Singin' in the Rain directed by Stanley Donen and Gene Kelly. Considered the best of all Hollywood movies, this Kelly-Debbie Reynolds-Donald O'Connor flick is still one of the funniest and sunniest views of the Hollywood Hills and the picture business.

High Noon directed by Fred Zinnemann. Remarkably conservative Gary Cooper (Oscar winner) starred in this deviously liberal tale of heroism in the face of disaster. Carl Foreman, later "blackballed" from the industry, wrote the screenplay. It showcased a very young actress from Philadelphia, Grace Kelly.

The Greatest Show on Earth directed by Cecil B. DeMille. Far from being what it claimed to be, this hugely entertaining movie was big, big, big. The cast, including James Stewart, Charlton Heston, Betty Hutton, and Gloria Grahame, was big. And so were the profits.

Three-D pictures make a brief pitch at wooing audiences. The 3-D glasses are cumbersome, and the fad quickly fades.

THE PLAYERS

Dean Martin and Jerry Lewis became America's favorite comic screen team, outpacing Abbott and Costello, in such shenanigans as *Jumping Jacks*.

Warner Brothers blonde Doris Day went from being a band singer to movie star with such hits as *April in Paris.*

In *Come Back, Little Sheba,* coquettish Terry Moore became the first actress since Lana Turner to make a career out of wearing a sweater.

MUSIC

"You Belong to Me" by Jo Stafford.

"Wheel of Fortune" by Kay Starr.

"I Went to Your Wedding" by Patti Page.

LITERATURE

Invisible Man by Ralph Ellison told the story of a disillusioned, idealistic black boy.

IN THE NEWS

Dwight David Eisenhower, the President of Columbia University, is selected as Republican standard-bearer for president. His choice of running mate is the highly esteemed Communist-hunter, Senator Richard M. Nixon from California. During the campaign Nixon is accused of misusing his funds. He goes on television with his famous "Checkers" speech. Checkers is the Nixon family dog. Nixon makes sure the country knows his wife Pat has only a "Republican cloth coat," nothing extravagant. Eisenhower/Nixon beat the democrats in November.

SPORTS

Julius Boros won the U.S. Open.

New York Yankees beat Brooklyn Dodgers 4–3 in the World Series.

Rocky Marciano won the heavyweight boxing championship.

TELEVISION

"Dragnet" starring Jack Webb arrived. Webb's dry delivery made him something of a cult classic. The detective stories were taken from real events.

Arthur Godfrey branched out with his second hit series, "Arthur Godfrey and His Friends."

Also Notable: Movie sidekick Eve Arden starred in "Our Miss Brooks"; Bandleader Ozzie Nelson brought his real family to the home screen in "The Adventures of Ozzie and Harriet" (they weren't very adventurous at all).

1953

THE MOVIES

From Here to Eternity directed by Fred Zinnemann. Based on James Jones's novel about Pearl Harbor, this all-star mega-hit had class. It also had Burt Lancaster and Deborah Kerr on the beach in a very memorable clinch. Montgomery Clift also starred. Oscars went, however, to good-girl-turned-bad Donna Reed and Frank Sinatra, whose career was saved by this powerhouse role. *Eternity* was the Best Picture of 1953.

Shane directed by George Stevens. Not only a big, grand Western, but every young boy's dream. A mysterious stranger comes to town and cleans out the bad guys; before he departs, he leaves behind the wisdom that the youth will need to survive as a man. This classic boasted Alan Ladd, Jean Arthur, young Brandon DeWilde, Van Heflin, and the meanest dog in movies, Jack Palance.

How to Marry a Millionaire directed by Jean Negulesco. Put three scheming women together looking for rich husbands, and you have a so-so movie. Now put reigning blonde Betty Grable together with soon-to-be goddess Marilyn Monroe, then add the purring Lauren Bacall and you have a big hit movie.

THE PLAYERS

Audrey Hepburn, a wafer-thin gossamer, grabbed attention of the American public in *Roman Holiday* and grabs the Oscar, too.

William Holden hit his stride in *Stalag 17.*

Frank Sinatra recaptured the early promise of his film career in *From Here to Eternity.* He arrived at the Oscar ceremonies with another nominee, his wife Ava Gardner, an Oscar loser for *Mogambo.*

MUSIC

Vaya Con Dios by Les Paul and Mary Ford.

Where is Your Heart by Percy Faith and his Orchestra.

You You You by the Ames Brothers.

IN THE NEWS

Unemployment was at postwar low, 2.9%.

Sir Edmund Hillary hit the heights of Mount Everest.

Julius and Ethel Rosenberg were executed as suspected spies at the height of Red-fever.

Desiderio Alberto Arnaz, IV, was born, but then again, so was Little Ricky Ricardo on "I Love Lucy." The ratings for the blessed event outdrew those for the inauguration of the president.

January 20: President Eisenhower and Vice President Nixon were sworn into office.

SPORTS

Racehorse Native Dancer won two of the three Triple Crown races, losing only the Kentucky Derby.

Maureen Connolly won all four women's tennis matches for a Grand Slam.

TELEVISION

Groucho Marx made his mark on television with his outrageous put downs on "You Bet Your Life." Snide and sarcastic, Groucho was an unusual, although lasting, TV star.

"Topper" starred Leo G. Carroll and two ghosts, Robert Sterling and Anne Jeffreys. The show was a spin-off of the popular film series, but never as clever.

1954

THE MOVIES

On the Waterfront directed by Elia Kazan. It's Brando at his most brilliant. He "coulda been a contender" in this tough and realistic portrayal of gangsters and regular, hardworking Joes. The Best Picture of 1954 concerned friends "ratting" on friends, a very potent topic in Hollywood and in the country during the McCarthy years. Brando won his first Oscar; costar Eva Marie Saint won a supporting statuette. Karl Malden, Rod Steiger, and Lee J. Cobb rounded out the cast.

The Country Girl directed by George Seaton. The glamorous Grace Kelly from Philadelphia played down her natural beauty as a frumpy wife to burned-out Bing Crosby. Some say Kelly stole the Oscar away from Judy Garland in *A Star is Born*, but Kelly did shine here. The ubiquitous and steady William Holden was on hand.

A Star is Born directed by George Cukor. This over-the-top musical featured Judy Garland in her come-back role. This was supposed to be the movie musical that rivaled *Gone with the Wind* for prestige. What it did was bomb at the box office. It is still a testament to a performer at her peak. It featured the reliable James Mason, Jack Carson, and Charles Bickford.

THE PLAYERS

It was Grace Kelly's year. She won the Oscar for *The Country Girl* and appeared in a succession of hit films: *Dial M for Murder,* and *Rear Window,* both directed by Alfred Hitchcock, and *Green Fire,* a far less successful addition to her filmography.

If Kelly was the hottest commodity in the country, no one told Mr. Marlon Brando who was putting his brand on nearly everything he touched. His method acting caused a sensation. His iconoclastic ways were completely un-Hollywood.

The complete star was Judy Garland, whose every move was recorded by gossip columnists, only because they were so erratic. The woman, talented in so many ways, allowed her neuroses to be filmed in *A Star is Born* to great advantage.

MUSIC

"Sh-Boom" by the Crew-Cuts.

"Wanted" by Perry Como.

"Three Coins in the Fountain" by the Four Aces from the movie of the same name.

IN THE NEWS

CBS reporter and journalist Edward R. Murrow exposed the tactics of Senator Joseph McCarthy's "witchhunt" for Communists.

The United States Supreme Court reversed itself and unanimously ruled in Brown vs. Board of Education that "separate but equal" was discriminatory.

General Motors introduced cars with 260-horsepower.

Sports legend Joe DiMaggio married screen star Marilyn Monroe in January. By October the couple called it quits.

The first McDonald's hamburger stand opened in DesPlaine, Illinois.

SPORTS

Roger Bannister was the first man to run the mile in less than four minutes. His time: 3:59:4.

Rocky Marciano defended his heavyweight title twice. He won both times.

San Francisco Giant Willie Mays robbed Indian Vic Wertz of an extra-base hit. The Giants go on to take the pennant from the Indians.

TELEVISION

"Father Knows Best" premiered and became synonymous with the average American family of the 1950s. The father was, as the title proclaimed, all knowing; the mother stayed home and cared for the family; the children were rambunctious, but finally controllable. Robert Young and Jane Wyatt were the parents; Elinor Donahue, Billy Gray, and Lauren Chapin were the children. Life was never really like this, but this show's impact was so strong that it made it seem as if it were true.

Ed Sullivan's "Toast of the Town" broke into the top ten ratings. Mr. Sullivan, always dour and ready to give a new act a try, captured Sunday nights for CBS.

1955

THE MOVIES

Rebel Without a Cause directed by Nicholas Ray. The teenager finally got a movie he and she could relate to. Juvenile delinquency, being a growing problem in the mid-50s, was the theme of this legendary film that brought James Dean to the forefront of the American scene. Alienated, disaffected, and confused, Dean was the 1950s Everyteenager. Then again, so were Natalie Wood and Sal Mineo.

The Blackboard Jungle directed by Richard Brooks. A frightening picture of violence in city schools, the film was based on the best-seller by Evan Hunter. Suddenly rock music was everywhere. "Rock Around the Clock" by Bill Haley and the Comets, which was played over the credits, ignited the country in controversy. The exposé starred Glenn Ford, Anne Francis, Sidney Poitier, and electrifying Vic Morrow.

Marty, directed by Delbert Mann. Alienation of another kind was evident in this Best Picture. A lonely butcher (Oscar winner Ernest Borgnine) might have been the adult version of the character played by Dean in *Rebel Without a Cause.* No one in *Marty* was able to fit in with the rest of society, much like Dean's vehicle. Loneliness and a sense of personal drift were making their way into the American psyche, much like heroism and purpose had their day during World War II.

Also Notable: *East of Eden* with James Dean; *Night of the Hunter* with Robert Mitchum; *The Seven Year Itch* with Marilyn Monroe and Tom Ewell.

THE PLAYERS

James Dean's leather jacket, jeans, and white T-shirt are still part of the American culture. His influence can be seen in actors on screen and television ever since he first burst onto the scene. *Rebel Without a Cause* did not only establish Dean in Hollywood, it made him a permanent member of the American family.

Natalie Wood's gang-girl image in *Rebel Without a Cause* was far from her first bit of fame. She was well-known since she was a little girl in films such as *Miracle on 34th Street,* but this film allowed her to transform herself into a major adult performer.

By the time Marilyn Monroe made *The Seven Year Itch,* she was firmly planted as an American icon. The billboard for the film in New York's Times Square put another notch in Monroe's famous belt. Her marriage and divorce from Joltin' Joe DiMaggio neither diminished her fame nor her ambition.

MUSIC

The song that brought the country to its feet was "Rock Around the Clock" by Bill Haley and the Comets.

The dramatic singing by Tennessee Ernie Ford made "Sixteen Tons" a big hit.

Children around the nation were singing along with Bill Hayes to "The Ballad of Davy Crockett," who was "the king of the wild frontier."

The cha-cha replaced other dance fads.

LITERATURE

Lord of the Rings by J. R. R. Tolkien mesmerized its first generation of readers.

The Man in the Gray Flannel Suit by Sloan Wilson typified a large section of the "establishment," hardworking, suburban professionals living seemingly pointless lives.

IN THE NEWS

President Eisenhower suffered a heart attack.

General Motors set a record $1 billion earnings.

Disneyland opened in Orange County, California.

The Salk Vaccine was developed.

SPORTS

Heavyweight boxing champion Rocky Marciano retired undefeated after two more bouts.

The Brooklyn Dodgers finally beat the Yankees for the World Series, the series making a hero out of Johnny Podres who threw two complete game wins over the boys in pinstripes.

Racehorse sensation Nashua won the Preakness and the Belmont Stakes, but lost the Kentucky Derby to Swaps in a major upset.

TELEVISION

"Alfred Hitchcock Presents," an anthology series hosted by the noted (and portly) director, premiered on October 2. Each week a new and unusual half-hour suspense drama was presented; the murder, madness, and mayhem were all gleeful jokes to the droll Mr. Hitchcock.

Game shows sweep the nation. Ardent fans watch every week as contestants vie for hundreds and thousands of dollars in cash and other merchandise. Among the most popular is "The $64,000 Question."

On CBS, the network with the highest rated shows, another radio performer becomes a television favorite, Jack Benny. His show featuring Don Wilson, Dennis Day, Eddie "Rochester" Anderson, and Mary Livingston displays all the foibles that made him so popular on the radio waves.

Disney took advantage of the publicity surrounding the opening of its amusement park in California and established itself on television with "Disneyland."

Jackie Gleason was a big star in every way. When his "The Honeymooners" premiered, he had no way of knowing the lasting nature of his character Ralph Kramden, his wife Alice, and his neighbors the Nortons. As with "I Love Lucy," one performer would not have been so notable without a fine supporting cast. In this case, Audrey Meadows, Joyce Randolph, and the vastly talented Art Carney rose to the occasion.

FADS AND FASHION

Poodle skirts and cinch waists were hot, hot, hot. So were the indispensable crinolines. The full-skirt look was perfect for dancing at the hop. For guys, the pompadour, leather jacket, and jeans seemed to be taken right off James Dean's back.

Older women were following Loretta Young, star of her own television series. Every week Miss Young would appear in another high-fashion outfit. She probably had as much influence on fashion as James Dean did. Just with a more upscale crowd.

TEEN IDOLS

When "The Mickey Mouse Club" opened its doors on October 3, 1955, Annette Funicello became one of the most popular of the Mouseketeers. Young girls idolized her, young boys lusted after her. It wasn't those mouse ears that made her famous either.

1956

THE MOVIES

Giant directed by George Stevens. Giant it was . . . and just plain big. Based on Edna Ferber's popular novel of the same name, this sprawling saga of the state of Texas had a formidable cast headed by Rock Hudson, Elizabeth Taylor, and James Dean as the irrepressible Jett Rink. Others involved in this terrible—if long—movie were Sal Mineo, Carroll Baker, and Dennis Hopper.

Around the World in Eighty Days directed by Michael Anderson. More importantly it was produced by the mega-showman Mike Todd, husband number three for Elizabeth Taylor. The film starred David Niven, Shirley MacLaine, and Cantinflas, but had nearly every big star in Hollywood in cameo appearances. In keeping with the flavor of the times, it was big, big, big. It sailed away with the Best Picture Oscar.

Baby Doll directed by Elia Kazan. When Tennessee Williams adapted his one-act play for the screen, he probably knew he was igniting a fire. Carroll Baker played the title role of a young bride who was being kept chaste until she turned the age of consent. Karl Malden was her too-patient husband, and Eli Wallach was his nemesis. There were uncomfortable laughs throughout, but this is a landmark film that pushed the envelope of acceptability.

Also Notable: Marilyn Monroe and Don Murray in the touching *Bus Stop,* in which the screen goddess proved once and for all that

27

she could act; John Ford's memorable *The Searchers;* the brilliant sci-fi masterpiece *The Invasion of the Body Snatchers.*

THE PLAYERS

Ingrid Bergman returned to the American screen. She had earlier been entangled in a scandalous affair while still married. Her triumphant return in *Anastasia* earned her the Oscar and an unyielding place in the hearts of most Americans.

Yul Brynner was not only the king of Siam in *The King and I* but was also featured in two other hot, hot films of the year: *The Ten Commandments* and *Anastasia.* He did for bald men what Ingrid Bergman did for women who loved men. Brynner was Best Actor for his monarch role.

Carroll Baker also had more than one hit. Her appearance as Rock Hudson and Elizabeth Taylor's daughter in *Giant* earned her recognition, but *Baby Doll* got her an Oscar nomination and a nickname that she would carry with her the rest of her life: Carroll "Baby Doll" Baker.

MUSIC

"Don't Be Cruel" by the boy whose hips swiveled, Elvis "The Pelvis" Presley.

"Whatever Will Be Will Be (*Que Será Será*)" by Doris Day from the Hitchcock film *The Man Who Knew Too Much.*

Carl Perkins's "Blue Suede Shoes" became an instant rock and roll classic.

Also Notable: Johnny Mathis's "Wonderful, Wonderful"; Fats Domino's deep-voiced "Ain't that a Shame"; one-of-a-kind artist Little Richard's "Long Tall Sally."

LITERATURE

"Howl" by Allen Ginsberg was the poetry of a new generation, one of disenchantment and alienation. What James Dean was to films, Ginsberg and his Beatniks were to the growing subculture of college-aged youth who felt separated from the mainstream. The world of coffeehouses and "deep" meaning, what some called pseudointellectualism, grew.

IN THE NEWS

In January a woman named Rosa Parks refused to sit in the back of a bus. She was arrested and fined. Parks, a black woman, stood up for her rights instead of sitting down in the back of that bus.

On April 19, screen queen Grace Kelly became Her Serene Royal Highness, Princess Grace of Monaco when the famous Philadelphian married Prince Rainier.

On April 23, the Supreme Court ruled that segregation in public transportation was unconstitutional.

The Republican team of Eisenhower and Nixon won easy reelection in November proving the slogan, "We Like Ike."

SPORTS

Mickey Mantle, the biggest star on the Yankees' lineup, won the Triple Crown with more home runs, RBIs, and a higher batting average than anyone in either league. Mantle may not have been the best fielder the team had, but he sure could hit a long ball.

Mantle teammate Don Larsen had the best game of his life in the fifth game of the World Series. He pitched the only perfect game in Series history.

Bobby Morrow was the first American to win two gold medals in Olympic competition since Jesse Owens in 1936. Morrow won his at the Melbourne games.

TELEVISION

An awkward columnist for a New York newspaper had been appearing on the air for some time. His show "Toast of the Town" had a name change. It was now called "The Ed Sullivan Show," and it became part of American lore to appear on the show. If you could make it there, you made it.

The low-key "December Bride," which starred character actress Spring Byington, was another CBS offering.

"General Electric Theatre" had as its host the former Warner Brothers contractee, Ronald Reagan. Like so many others in the film world, he answered when opportunity knocked.

On July 9, Dick Clark became the official host of "American Bandstand." Whatever the music, Clark seemed to be in touch with it.

1957

THE MOVIES

Peyton Place directed by Mark Robson. Taken from the scandalous novel by Grace Metalious, this story of small-town intrigue and hidden lusts is just what audiences were looking for—contrived soap opera with serious undertones. Lana Turner finally got a role that allowed her to act. The all-star cast included Russ Tamblyn, David Nelson (from TV's Ozzie and Harriet), Arthur Kennedy, and Hope Lange.

Love Me Tender directed by Robert D. Webb. Elvis hit the screen and made a big impression. While he was no threat to Brando, his own brand of sex appeal was good enough to fill theatres across the country. His costars Debra Paget and Richard Egan were along for the ride.

12 Angry Men directed by Sidney Lumet. In his first film directing job, Lumet showed that he could handle not only a large veteran cast, but more importantly a tough issue of blind justice gone amok. Henry Fonda, Ed Begley, E.G. Marshall, and other notable character actors of the day squabbled as the jurors.

Also Notable: *The Bridge on the River Kwai* with ever-reliable William Holden and Oscar-winning Alec Guinness plus one of the most whistled movie themes of all time. Kwai was 1957's Best Picture; *Sweet Smell of Success,* and Billy Wilder's *Witness for the Prosecution* attracted audiences.

THE PLAYERS

Joanne Woodward showed just what kind of versatile actress she was with *The Three Faces of Eve*. Her marriage to Paul Newman made headlines, and she was recognized as Best Actress of the year.

For every boy like Elvis Presley, there was a boy like Pat Boone, who had the clean-cut image parents liked. Boone was no Elvis, but he had a string of hit films like *April Love*.

Of course the real thing, Elvis, made a big impression in *Love Me Tender* and *Jailhouse Rock*.

MUSIC

"Wake Up Little Susie" by the melodious Everly Brothers put the duo somewhere between the raciness of Elvis and the sugar-coated Pat Boone.

Elvis, the King, sang "All Shook Up," and that's what happened to his legions of fans.

Pat Boone, the younger version of Perry Como, came out on top with "April Love."

Also Notable: Harry Belafonte's "Banana Boat Song," the hit that followed him the rest of his career; Buddy Holly and the Crickets' "That'll Be the Day," and Jerry Lee Lewis's "Whole Lotta Shakin' Goin' On," a song that really never went out of style in rock music.

LITERATURE

Doctor Zhivago by Boris Pasternak told the story of the Russian Revolution through very sympathetic characters, but was banned in the Soviet Union.

On the opposite side of the world—in more ways than one—was Jack Kerouac's *On The Road* a tribute to loneliness and alienation. Writer Truman Capote, in reviewing the Beat Generation's bible, called it "typewriting."

IN THE NEWS

Federally mandated school integration was resisted by Arkansas Governor Orval Faubus. Federal troops had to be sent in.

On September 9, President Eisenhower signed the first Civil Rights Act since the Grant administration in the mid-nineteenth century.

SPORTS

Stan "The Man" Musial batted an astounding .351 in his seven teenth year in baseball.

Both the New York Giants and the Brooklyn Dodgers announced that they were leaving the East Coast for the land of opportunity, California.

Althea Gibson, called the "slim Harlem" tennis star by patronizing sports writers, was the first black to win at Wimbledon. The "girl" from Harlem accepted her award from England's Queen Elizabeth II.

TELEVISION

"The $64,000 Question" is just one of many popular TV games shows. It was this one, though, that had infamy dumped on its fame with the exposure of rigging. Charles Van Doren, of the prominent writing family, came to fame as the patsy who made good.

"Gunsmoke" starred James Arness as Marshal Matt Dillon and Amanda Blake as Miss Kitty. This Western was the biggest of its kind on the tube, but there were others: "Tales of Wells Fargo" and "Have Gun Will Travel," among others.

Narrated by reporter Walter Winchell, "The Untouchables" was a violent, corpse-ridden show about the noted Chicago crime-fighter Eliot Ness and his men who went after Al Capone. Bloody, yes, but entertaining, too. Robert Stack was emotionless as Ness; perhaps his stunned expression was an indication he was shocked to be working as an actor. The show debuted on November 15, produced by DesiLu.

Also Notable: "The Danny Thomas Show" with the entertainer playing a blustery nightclub singer; "I've Got a Secret" with its famous panel of mini-celebrities. On October 4, *Leave it to Beaver*" moved onto America's television block. We've been friends since.

FADS AND FASHION

Ford introduced its Edsel, a very clumsy, clunky design that no one liked very much. It became a symbol of how things can go wrong, and its very name has made its way into the language as a synonym for failure.

The "Bag" look in women's fashion made its way across the wide Atlantic and made American women look as wide as the sea.

A homegrown product, the Frisbee, began showing up on college campuses and soon everywhere else. The origins of the flying disc are shrouded in mystery—or at least lies—but the saucer has been lots of fun.

1958

THE MOVIES

Cat on a Hot Tin Roof directed by Richard Brooks. This was no "puss and boots" story. Tennessee Williams's tale of greed and lies and Southern misery was dished up in a terrific stew. Elizabeth Taylor and Paul Newman played a married couple with a terrible secret. Of course, it was not quite so terrible in the film version as it was on stage. Still, the subject matter of homosexuality was not something everyone was comfortable with in 1958.

The Defiant Ones directed by socially conscious Stanley Kramer. Again, a topic otherwise abhorrent to audiences was gussied up and made sellable. This story was about a white man and a black man shackled together as they tried to escape the law. It proved to everyone what only a few were willing to admit: People are more alike than different. Tony Curtis and Sidney Poitier taught us that valuable lesson.

There was some fun at the movies: *Auntie Mame* directed by Morton DaCosta. Rosalind Russell pulled out all the stops, but she, too, was a socially-correct woman, just one with money. While always entertaining, the movie got in a few well-placed jabs, especially at the Eisenhowers. Peggy Cass and Roger Smith were featured players.

Also Notable: Hitchcock's *Vertigo,* one of the most emulated movies ever; Orson Welles's deeply disturbing *Touch of Evil;* the

realistic *I Want to Live!* with a powerhouse Oscar performance by
Susan Hayward.

THE PLAYERS

Elizabeth Taylor was the recent widow of her third husband, the
late Mike Todd, but she still reigned at the box office.

Lana Turner turned tragedy into a career. After her daughter Cheryl
Crane stabbed Lana's boyfriend to death, the actress appeared in
films that exploited the situation.

The Rat Pack grabbed headlines. Frank Sinatra, Dean Martin,
Sammy Davis, Jr., Shirley MacLaine, Joey Bishop, and Peter Law-
ford belonged to a group of entertainers who kept each other entertained. They starred in movies together, such as 1958's *Some Came
Running* or they appeared in Las Vegas together or just drank together.

MUSIC

Television star Ricky Nelson became record star Ricky Nelson. His
"Poor Little Fool" went to the top of the charts.

Instrumental hit "Tequila" by the Champs was a sales champ.

Nel Blu Dipinto Di Blu (Volare) by Domingo Modugno had everybody humming the melody of this instrumental.

Also Notable: the novelty hit "The Purple People Eater"; Danny
and the Juniors' "At the Hop"; the incomparable Jerry Lee Lewis's
"Great Balls of Fire"; Buddy Holly's "Peggy Sue."

LITERATURE

Lolita by Vladimir Nabokov gave new meaning to the words
Maurice Chevalier sang in the year's Best Picture, *Gigi:* "Thank

heaven for little girls." The story of a much older man obsessed with a teen became part of American lore.

IN THE NEWS

On January 31, the first U.S. satellite to go into orbit, *Explorer,* was launched by the Army.

The first domestic jet airline passenger service in the country was opened by National Airlines. On December 10, the route between New York and Miami was open.

Don't leave home without them: Both BankAmerica and American Express cards were introduced.

SPORTS

UCLA's Rafer Johnson won big at the Moscow games. He set a world record in the decathlon, earning 8,302 points.

In the "greatest football game" ever played, the Baltimore Colts beat the New York Giants 23 to 17. The excitement lasted into overtime and had a one-yard plunge for the goal by Alan Ameche.

In horse racing, Tim Tam won the Kentucky Derby.

TELEVISION

Westerns were everywhere. Old saddle-tramp actor Ward Bond led the "Wagon Train" on NBC, while over on CBS former athlete Chuck Connors was "The Rifleman." Richard Boone was Palladin, the mysterious gunslinger in "Have Gun, Will Travel." Other notable shows: "Maverick" with James Garner; "Sugarfoot"; Clint Walker in "Cheyenne"; Gene Barry as the dashing "Bat Masterson."

FADS AND FASHION

Fifteen million hula hoops were sold to an avid population who wanted to swing their hips, perhaps emulating Elvis or perhaps because statehood for Hawaii was on so many people's minds.

She was beautiful; she was blonde; she was plastic. And anyone could buy her. She was Barbie. Mattel Toys introduced her and she's been changing outfits with the American scene ever since.

1959

THE MOVIES

Some Like It Hot directed by Billy Wilder. One of the funniest movies ever made doesn't sound like one: Two down-and-out musicians witness the St. Valentine's Day Massacre and have to leave Chicago. They disguise themselves as women to join an all-girl band. There they meet the lead singer, Sugar Kane. Macho men in drag was one thing, but this comedy pushed even further and was condemned by many religious groups. Jack Lemmon, Tony Curtis, and Marilyn Monroe were never better, while Wilder's direction and writing have hardly been equalled.

Anatomy of a Murder directed by Otto Preminger. Seldom had a movie been this frank in the details of murder. Basically a court-room drama, the realism and grit were also new to moviegoing audiences. With James Stewart playing it straight, the cast also included Lee Remick, George C. Scott, and Eve Arden.

North by Northwest directed by Alfred Hitchcock. This movie was designed to be the ultimate Hitchcock thrill by screenwriter Ernest Lehman. The premise was simple: An innocent man was being pursued by both the "good" guys and the "bad." As that innocent man, Cary Grant was totally elegant as he tried to get out of some of the most dangerous situations committed to film, including the great sequence of ducking a murderous crop duster. Along for the ride were Eva Marie Saint, James Mason, and Martin Landau.

Also Notable: The epic *Ben-Hur* with ever-stoic Charlton Heston. It won eleven Oscars; *Porgy and Bess,* based on the Gershwin opera; the end-of-the-world tale *On the Beach.*

THE PLAYERS

Married to one of America's foremost playwrights and at the height (while alive) of her fame, Marilyn Monroe had never sparkled quite so radiantly as she did in *Some Like It Hot.* Young boys across the country asked their mothers to invite the blonde for dinner. Plenty of older men dreamed the same thoughts.

Doris Day and Rock Hudson were America's clean-cut couple, an arranged marriage of career convenience that gave both parties the lift they needed. In *Pillow Talk* he pursued her virtue while, at times, pretending not to be interested in women.

Cary Grant had two sensational hits: *North by Northwest* and *Operation Petticoat.* But his presence was felt in a third. His *Operation Petticoat* costar, Tony Curtis, did an extended imperson-ation of Grant in *Some Like It Hot.* One of that movie's gags had Jack Lemmon saying to Curtis, "Nobody talks like that."

MUSIC

Frank Sinatra-wannabe Bobby Darin slashed his way to the top of the charts with "Mack the Knife." The singer had plans to act—on the screen and off—just like his idol, "Old Blue Eyes" from Hoboken, Sinatra.

Johnny Horton had an unusual hit. Its lyrics were all about Colonel Andrew Jackson and the British during the War of 1812. The song, "The Battle of New Orleans," topped the charts.

Perennial college favorite "Charlie Brown" was sung by the Coasters.

Also Notable: Philadelphia boy, Frankie Avalon, hit the big time with "Venus"; Connie Francis was singing "Lipstick on Your Collar"; Edd Byrnes of "77 Sunset Strip" had a hit with "Kookie, Kookie, Lend Me Your Comb."

On February 3, Buddy Holly and the Big Bopper died in a plane crash.

LITERATURE

Allen Drury's *Advise and Consent* sent people into bookstores to get the dirt on the dirty doings in Washington, D.C.

IN THE NEWS

Flag companies went wild: On January 3, Alaska was admitted into the union. On August 31, Hawaii became the fiftieth state. Anticipating these events and following them, America celebrated in a variety of ways: movies (*North to Alaska, Blue Hawaii*), television (*Hawaiian Eye*), and, of course, the hula hoop.

The St. Lawrence Seaway was opened on April 25.

Between September 15 and 27, Soviet Premier Nikita Khrushchev took a transcontinental tour of America, ending in Hollywood where he was feted by our equivalent of royalty.

SPORTS

For the first time since 1934, a European had won the heavyweight championship. Ingemar Johansson beat American Floyd Patterson for the title.

Lee Perry was judged the winner of the Daytona 500 in a photo finish. The problem: No photo finish camera in Daytona.

The Chicago White Sox went down to defeat at the hands and gloves of the new Los Angeles team, the Dodgers.

TELEVISION

From the soundstage of Warner Brothers studios . . . thus began many a detective show. The young stock company at the studio included Efrem Zimbalist, Jr., Roger Smith, Connie Stevens, Edd Byrnes, and Robert Conrad. The shows they appeared in were all set in somewhat exotic locations, such as Hawaii or on Sunset Strip. The shows, "Hawaiian Eye," "Surfside Six," and "77 Sunset Strip" were all forgettable but easy to watch.

Another former movie personality made it big on the small screen. His name was Red Skelton and his antics were unforgettable. His variety show featured guest stars and comic skits. His roster of characters included Clem Kadiddlehopper, Freddie the Freeloader, and "Gertrude and Heathcliff," two very stupid sea gulls. Anyone know a smart sea gull?

It wasn't just for the kids: "Rocky and his Friends" premiered on September 29. The cartoon characters from Frost Bite Falls and their zany pals were fun enough for children, but the writing was aimed at a much larger audience. They all laughed.

FADS AND FASHION

The bikini was opening the eyes of the American male to the benefits of going to the beach.

THE
1960s

It was a time of laughter and a time of tears. It was an era of possibilities and an era of possibilities lost. It was a springtime of great expectations and a fall of greater disappointments. It was the 1960s, the tumultuous years from which America will never totally recover

Elected president in the fall of 1960, John F. Kennedy presided over the momentous shift of power to a younger generation. The president's own perceived vitality and movie-star good looks reinvigorated the nation. His election ushered in a new era of politics by personal style. It was not enough, as Kennedy's rival Richard Nixon was, to be young. It was not enough to have an attractive wife and children. *Charm* was essential.

With the new President Kennedy in office, America seemed a different place. Children were encouraged by the President's Council on Physical Fitness to get into and stay in shape. The fine arts were supported as never before: The new president and his wife entertained Nobel Prize winners in the White House. Culture was on the move again. New boundaries were being set. The volunteer organizations, Peace Corps and VISTA (Volunteers in Service to America) were set in motion. Suddenly helping others less fortunate mattered. America was setting a good example.

America's youth now had their own anthem: rock and roll. Elvis Presley may have been the embodiment of this new music, but he was not alone. Joining him as musical influences on the young were such trendsetters as Chuck Berry, Little Richard, Jerry Lee Lewis, and Carl Perkins. Out of Detroit came the Motown sound, Berry Gordy's talented stable of stars: The Supremes, The Temptations, Martha Reeves and the Vandellas, and many more.

America's young president was challenged at home and abroad. While the Civil Rights movement gained momentum, attentions were diverted by the Bay of Pig's fiasco wherein the American government backed Cuban refugees in their attempt to invade their homeland. The invasion failed ignominiously on April 17, 1961. Cuban leader Fidel Castro has secured power.

John Kennedy's assassination stunned the nation and the world. The bloom was forever off the rose. It was only the beginning of the disillusionment that was to follow throughout the decade.

No man was ever so awkward as Lyndon Baines Johnson as he ascended to the presidency. He was an awkward man in an awkward situation. His gracelessness contrasted sharply with the ease of his predecessor. However, LBJ was one of the most astute practitioners of the political game. While his physical appearance and demeanor seemed off-kilter, he dominated Congress like few men before or since.

The war in Southeast Asia escalated, and with that growth came antiwar demonstrations.

Civil unrest, too, grew as a result of racial strife. Riots broke out in Newark, Detroit, and Los Angeles, among other cities and towns.

Johnson's grip on the presidency was as slippery as the issue of Vietnam. When Senator Eugene McCarthy made what seemed to be a successful bid against him for the Democratic presidential nomination in 1968, Johnson's days were numbered.

In April 1968, Reverend Martin Luther King, Jr., was assassinated in Memphis. His nonviolent stand on Civil Rights had won him the Nobel Peace Prize.

In June 1968, Senator Robert F. Kennedy was assassinated in Los Angeles. He had, moments earlier, delivered his victory speech having won the California primary. The dream of a second Kennedy presidency evaporated.

The deaths of these two men dashed the hopes and prayers of many. America was going through growing pains, and these men symbolized a comfortable growth to maturity. They spoke to and for "the people." Without them and their dreams for a better society, there was only more fear.

In 1964 America was rocked by something else. Like no musical group before or after, there were the Beatles. Beatlemania swept the nation. This new brand of rock and roll was here to stay.

Soon after the Beatles came the much more *dangerous* Rolling
Stones who exalted sexuality further than Elvis thought possible.
At least on television things were safe. For a while. The family
situation comedies of the 1950s were replaced with the family situation comedies of the 1960s; they were still gentle diversions. Ed
Sullivan never varied. Lucille Ball was back and up to her old
tricks. But television could not resist the radical mood swings of
the era. "That Was the Week that Was" was among the first shows
ever to *criticize* official government policy. And they got away with
it. However not enough viewers tuned in week after week to watch
the irreverency. By 1968 audiences were ready for something completely different. It was "Rowan and Martin's Laugh-In."

Cassius Clay began the decade as a star athlete of the Olympics.
By the end of the 1960s he was Muhammed Ali, the Heavyweight
Boxing Champion of the World. What he lacked in modesty he
made up for in sheer athletic talent.

The big joke of major league baseball was the expansion team
from New York, the hapless Mets. As with everything else that occurred in the 1960s, anything was possible. And so it was in 1969
the New York Mets actually won the World Series.

In November 1968, the nation elected former Vice President
Richard M. Nixon as President of the United States. The thirty-
seventh president was a man who stood squarely in the middle of
the road. It is where the country hoped to remain.

1960

THE MOVIES

Journey to the Center of the Earth directed by Henry Levin. This otherwise standard Hollywood fare was enhanced by special effects. Especially entertaining for kids, the old Jules Verne story of an adventurer who travels to the Earth's core starred James Mason, Arlene Dahl, and Pat Boone.

The Apartment directed by Billy Wilder. America was getting more sophisticated because of writer/director Wilder's acerbic view of our culture's mores. Here he attacked traditional corporate life, the shenanigans that allow people to get ahead, and immorality. Heady stuff, for sure, to a people more used to "The Mickey Mouse Club." Jack Lemmon, Shirley MacLaine, and Fred MacMurray (in a very un-Fred MacMurray role) were all great in this Best Picture of 1960.

Spartacus directed by Stanley Kubrick. This is the movie that broke the Hollywood blacklist on writers when producer/star Kirk Douglas hired a former Red-scare victim. This was always the thinking man's spectacle with a literate script, fine performances from an all-star cast, and terrific photography. It was odd having Tony Curtis and Laurence Olivier giving each other the eye. Peter Ustinov won the Supporting Actor nod.

Also Notable: *Elmer Gantry, Inherit the Wind,* and Hitchcock's unique *Psycho.*

THE PLAYERS

Anthony Perkins gave the performance of his life as Norman Bates in *Psycho*. Neither he nor the film have left the public consciousness since the film opened.

The former Alexandra Zuck, now Sandra Dee, was the darling of Hollywood. Her storybook marriage to Bobby Darin kept the two in the public eye while she went from one light comedy to another. After all, Miss Dee was the original *Gidget*.

Sal Mineo had been a strange teen actor who graduated to bigger stuff in his role in the film *Exodus*. His unique looks made him the heartthrob of young girls, even if his moment was fleeting.

MUSIC

Chubby Checker's "The Twist" gave the country something to twist and shout about. A new dance craze was born.

If the War of 1812 was good enough to base a song on, how about working on a chain gang? Many who listened to Sam Cooke's "Working on a Chain Gang" did not realize the storyline.

"Only the Lonely (Know How I Feel)" by Roy Orbison was another of the singer's operatic ballads. What Orbison sang sounded as if it came directly from his heart.

Also Notable: another novelty tune, "Itsy Bitsy Teenie Weenie Yellow Polka Dot Bikini," kept up with the fashion trends; "Sink the Bismarck," about doing just that during World War II; Percy Faith's "Theme from A Summer Place" and "North to Alaska," the forty-ninth state.

LITERATURE

To Kill a Mockingbird by Harper Lee became an instant American classic and is taught in high schools all over. The story of a stand-up-and-take-action kind of guy, Atticus Finch, was told through the eyes of his adoring young daughter. Finch defended a black man falsely accused of a crime.

IN THE NEWS

On May 1, a U.S. reconnaissance plane was shot down over the Soviet Union.

The presidential debates between Vice President Richard M. Nixon and Senator John F. Kennedy were televised. Kennedy won, most say, because of his telegenic personality. Those who listened on the radio felt that the Vice President won.

The population explosion worried many who felt the world was getting too small. Pregnancy control was advised.

On April 1, the U.S. launched its first weather satellite.

In November, the Democratic slate of John Kennedy and Lyndon Johnson narrowly beat Republicans Richard Nixon and Henry Cabot Lodge. If only one more Republican per voting district had voted, the outcome would have been different.

SPORTS

Golfer Arnold Palmer was in good form. He won an astounding eight of the twenty-seven tournaments he entered, including the Masters and the U.S. Open.

You can do it, if you try: Wilma Rudolph, who had polio as a child, won three gold medals at the Rome Olympics for sprinting.

Taciturn Ted Williams of the Boston Red Sox retired at the age of forty-two with a career batting average of .344. Many believe he was the greatest hitter of all time. He left the game in a big way, hitting a homer at his last at bat.

TELEVISION

Down-home was the trend. "The Andy Griffith Show" was set in fictional Mayberry, a place that many Americans still wish existed. "The Real McCoys" had the benefit of veteran actor Walter Brennan and much younger, but still a veteran, Richard Crenna, late of "Our Miss Brooks."

"The Flintstones" were really a knock-off of "The Honeymooners," but kids of all ages still loved the Stone Age gang. The show premiered on September 30.

FADS AND FASHION

Chic was Elizabeth Taylor in a black low-cut dress in the awful film from John O'Hara's novel *Butterfield 8*.

College kids were trying to find out how many people they could jam into a telephone booth.

Those old 78 rpm records were replaced by the stackable, less clunky 45 rpm records. The big hole in the middle was never explained.

TEEN IDOLS

Tuesday Weld was young and beautiful and on the hit TV show "Dobie Gillis," but she never seemed innocent, even as a teenager. There was something sexually alive in her portrayal of Thalia Menninger. It was this spark that attracted her fans. Behind her wide eyes was the brilliance of the actress she would become.

1961

THE MOVIES

West Side Story directed by Robert Wise and Jerome Robbins. The musicalized *Romeo and Juliet* was set on New York's upper West Side. Instead of feuding families, it featured rival gangs. While many found it hard to believe that gangs in New York would sing and dance like the ones in this movie, the performances were wonderful. When Oscar-winning Rita Moreno and Oscar recipient George Chakiri sang about what it was like to be Puerto Ricans "in America," it taught the audience a few things.

The Hustler directed by Robert Rossen. The grit and grime of professional pool playing was not something that seemed likely to lure audiences. But reality was setting in and people were enjoying it. Paul Newman was at his most disaffected. He was callous; he was mean; he was sexy. Also shooting from the hip were George C. Scott and TV funny man Jackie Gleason as the real-life Minnesota Fats.

The Disney movies: *The Absent-Minded Professor* and *The Parent Trap*. Families went to these movies in droves. Fred MacMurray invented Flubber in the firs, and America discovered British Hayley Mills in the second.

Also Notable: the highly dramatic *Judgment at Nuremberg, Breakfast at Tiffany's* with Audrey Hepburn as Holly Golightly, and *Two Women* imported from Italy.

THE PLAYERS

Natalie Wood had been a favorite teen star in such films as *Rebel Without a Cause*. As she matured, the public followed her, mostly because she was in an archetypical Hollywood marriage to "dream boat" actor Robert Wagner. But when Wood gave double-whammy performances in *West Side Story* and *Splendor in the Grass,* she wasn't just a gossip item any more. However, she didn't lose her touch in that department either. Her romance with *Splendor* costar Warren Beatty kept her "image" as one sexy woman alive.

Paul Newman had been a star for a decade. His marriage to Joanne Woodward was very different from Wood and Wagner's. The Newmans kept a low profile, but Newman's talent was getting more of the attention it deserved. *The Hustler* made him a house-hold name.

Sophia Loren won an Oscar for her role in *Two Women,* the first ever for a foreign language film. Having been in the United States for several other films, she was not a new commodity. From this point on, she was an international star.

MUSIC

"Big Bad John" was about a coal mining accident. Another great idea for a hit song. It was by Jimmy Dean.

"Runaround Sue" by Dion didn't get the runaround from fans. It went to the top of the charts.

"Running Bear" by Johnny Preston had fathers worried about their daughters. The song was about two young Indians who fell in love and died while trying to swim to one another.

Also Notable: Ben E. King's "Stand by Me"; Gary Bonds (who inserted "U.S." as a middle name) had a hit with "Quarter to Three";

the incomparable Ray Charles wailed away on "Hit the Road Jack."

LITERATURE

Ernest Hemingway committed suicide, just as his father had done, in Ketchum, Idaho.

IN THE NEWS

On January 20, a cold and snowy day in Washington, D.C., the new president was inaugurated. His vision for the future was called "The New Frontier." He and his beautiful and charming wife brought American culture into the White House as it hadn't been revered in some time. It was his father's money that brought him to office; it was his own style that made him adored by so many.

On April 17, the "Bay of Pigs'" invasion of Cuba was a fiasco for the new administration and for democracy in the Western Hemisphere.

Commander Alan B. Shepard, Jr., was the first man into suborbital space. He was launched on May 5 from Cape Canaveral, Florida.

On August 13, the Berlin Wall went up. With it came the chilliest era of the Cold War.

A new federal agency, the Peace Corps, went into effect to train Americans to help underdeveloped nations. Kennedy brother-in-law Sargent Shriver was the first administrator.

Sniffing glue by youths had grown to epidemic proportions.

SPORTS

It was the upside-down year—1961. Roger Maris and Mickey Mantle were locked in a fierce battle to see who would end the season with the most homers. By the end of the season, it was Maris who beat Babe Ruth's record. The entire Yankees, however, had totalled a whopping 240 home runs among them.

The Green Bay Packers led by the much admired Vince Lombardi trounced the New York Giants for the NFL title. The final score: Green Bay 37, New York 0.

On March 13, Floyd Patterson, defended his heavyweight crown and knocked out Ingemar Johansson for the championship.

TELEVISION

The doctors take to the air: "Dr. Kildare," starring Richard Chamberlain, and "Ben Casey," starring Vince Edwards, both appeared for the first time.

"Perry Mason" solved cases week after week, making mincemeat of his usual opponent, Hamilton (Ham?) Burger. Raymond Burr and Barbara Hale starred.

On NBC, "Hazel" was holding court. The feisty domestic was played with charm by Broadway and movie actress Shirley Booth.

On CBS, a more sophisticated brand of humor was served up with "The Dick Van Dyke Show," starring the rubbery faced comedian and Mary Tyler Moore as his wife Laura. These people actually looked like they were in love with each other. Although it was against the censor's wishes, it seemed like they had sex and enjoyed it.

FADS AND FASHIONS

Bomb shelters were being built to protect us from a growing list of enemies.

The Kennedys were fashion. Unlike other First Ladies, Mrs. Kennedy cared about how she looked at all times. Her bouffant hair and classic A-line skirts were imitated everywhere.

1962

THE MOVIES

What Ever Happened to Baby Jane? directed by Robert Aldrich. Bette Davis and Joan Crawford were two old movie queens who played two old movie queens. Most studios thought ill of the idea, but Warner Brothers, their old lot, backed the low-budget gothic and everybody made a mint. This sleeper was good news for old queens everywhere. They were back in business—several cheapie thrillers came about because of Baby Jane.

Dr. No directed by Terence Young. Sean Connery was "Bond, James Bond." Martinis were shaken, not stirred, but the audience was. Suddenly movies were really thrilling, shot on locations with camera tricks and women who knew how to wear bikinis. Ursula Andress never had to do another film to be remembered forever for her stunning entrance. It was a foreign production for all-American men.

To Kill a Mockingbird directed by Robert Mulligan. As the sincere Atticus Finch, Gregory Peck had found the role that used his sullenness to good advantage. He was honored as Best Actor for his role of a white lawyer who defends an innocent black man. It could have been taken from the headlines of the daily newspapers.

Also Notable: The magnificent Best Picture *Lawrence of Arabia* was grandly sweeping across the nation; *The Days of Wine and*

Roses, uncorked a view of a two-alcoholic marriage; *Bird Man of Alcatraz* with Burt Lancaster; *The Manchurian Candidate* about a man programmed to kill the president.

THE PLAYERS

Peter O'Toole had been the second choice to star as Lawrence of Arabia. The first was Marlon Brando, but the American's decision to turn it down made an international star of little-known O'Toole.

She rose from the dead: Bette Davis's career had been reduced to making guest appearances on "Wagon Train," a big come-down for a two-time Oscar winner. And although she was in a trashy movie, it was a big hit.

Katharine Hepburn, Davis's most enduring competition in the old days, never took the low-down road: In 1962 she appeared in *Long Day's Journey into Night,* and proved to be an actress of serious emotional depth.

MUSIC

Donna Reed's television daughter Shelley Fabares hit the charts with "Johnny Angel."

Gene Chandler's "Duke of Earl," was a doo-wop hit.

"Telstar" by the Tornadoes exulted in the promise of space travel.

Also Notable: The twist had several new variations. "The Peppermint Twist," which was named after the chic New York club The Peppermint Lounge where even the Duke and Duchess of Windsor were seen dancing. The Four Seasons had several big singles, "Big Girls Don't Cry" and "Sherry."

LITERATURE

Silent Spring by Rachel Carson was one of the first books to draw the public's attention to matters of ecology. Were we really polluting our air and water for the sake of industry?

Sex and the Single Girl by *Cosmopolitan* magazine editor Helen Gurley Brown taught young women how to handle money—earned by the rich men that they landed!

IN THE NEWS

On February 20, John Glenn became the first American to orbit the earth.

Guerrilla warfare was spreading in a small, faraway place in Asia. The place was called Vietnam.

The space race was a heated issue—who would land on the moon first? Would it be the United States or arch foe, the Soviet Union?

June 11, 1962, the Anglin brothers and Frank Williams did the impossible. They escaped from Alcatraz.

President Kennedy averted a U.S. Steel strike.

On Sunday morning August 5, the news reported the death of Marilyn Monroe. The exact nature of the woman's death has been a constant source of mystery and profit for many. What she left behind, besides her worldly possessions, was an enormous amount of joy.

Former Vice President Nixon ran against Edmund "Pat" Brown for the governor-ship of California. Nixon lost and told reporters that they "wouldn't have Nixon to kick around any more," promising his retirement.

In October, the Cuban Missile Crisis sent fear throughout the country. Families went to sleep, after hearing the president's strong words on television, believing there would be no morning.

SPORTS

Dodger Maury Wills broke Ty Cobb's single-season stolen base record. Philadelphia Warrior Wilt Chamberlain scored one hundred points in one game. He reached that mark with only forty-eight seconds remaining to play.

Heavyweight champ Floyd Patterson was KO'd by Sonny Liston in a fight that didn't last two minutes.

The New York Mets were the losingest team around—they were beaten in 120 games.

TELEVISION

Ben Cartwright and his three sons dominated Sunday nights on NBC. "Bonanza" was just that for Lorne Greene, Dan Blocker, Pernell Roberts, and Michael Landon.

Lucy was back but without Desi. "The Lucy Show" starred the famous red-head and her constant sidekick Vivian Vance, but it was in most ways a pale imitation of "I Love Lucy." Still, Lucille Ball could have appeared in anything and have had big ratings.

"The Beverly Hillbillies" was a phenomenon. Old Jed Clampett had struck oil and headed for the hills . . . of Beverly. Along with Irene Ryan as Granny, Donna Douglas as Ellie Mae, and Max Baer, Jr., as Jethro, Jed (Buddy Ebsen) had to learn what to do with success. A very funny show.

TEEN IDOLS

Fabian was a singer from Philadelphia just like Frankie Avalon, but Frankie was the boy next door. Fabian had a much darker personality. It caught fire when the young singer acted on an episode of "Bus Stop" in 1962. His overt sexuality was such a threat, he and the show were criticized by the Catholic Church. The show left the airwaves; Fabian's hot career flickered.

1963

THE MOVIES

The Birds directed by Alfred Hitchcock. The world was out of balance, and no one could save it. Nature had taken its own course to correct the imbalance. Frightening and prescient, *The Birds* was an environmentalist's dream, long before there were such things. Tippi Hedren, Rod Taylor, Suzanne Pleshette, and Jessica Tandy headed up another Hitchcock masterpiece.

Tom Jones directed by Tony Richardson. Bawdy and ripe, juicy and delicious, *Tom Jones* was like nothing ever before seen on the screen. Never had the mere act of eating looked so sexy. In fact everything about this movie was sexy. And everybody kept their clothes on. With Albert Finney, Diane Cilento, and Dame Edith Evans, the British certainly taught Americans a few things. We reciprocated by naming it Best Picture.

Cleopatra directed by Joseph L. Mankiewicz. Not a very good movie, but an experience all the same. Literally years in the making, probably no movie in the history of film ever got so much publicity before it opened. And that was simply because Elizabeth Taylor had ditched her fourth husband, crooner Eddie Fisher, during the production and proclaimed to the world that she was in love with costar Richard Burton.

Also Notable: Paul Newman in *Hud,* playing a real stinker of a guy; the all-star *The Great Escape; How the West Was Won* in

63

Cinerama, a wide-screen experience like no other; the extremely funny and extremely-all-star *It's a Mad, Mad, Mad, Mad World.*

THE PLAYERS

Elizabeth Taylor and Richard Burton were the world's most famous lovers. Virtually, their every move was captured on film, including nudes of her taken with a telephoto lens. The uproar about their romance caused the biggest scandal since Ingrid Bergman met Roberto Rossellini.

Ann-Margret was just a starlet but she was making quite an impression with films such as *Bye Bye Birdie.*

MUSIC

She wore "Blue Velvet" in Bobby Vinton's hit of the same name. He had a habit of having colors in the names of his songs: "Blue on Blue," "Roses are Red," etc.

The college favorite "Louie Louie" went to the top of the charts for the Kingsmen.

As their name suggested Ruby and the Romantics were certainly exciting. They had a big one with "Our Day Will Come."

Bob Dylan's *Freewheelin'* was his first album to hit the charts.

Also Notable: The surfing sounds of the Beach Boys, the California group who had the hit "Surfin' USA"; the sounds of the Singing Nun who sang "Dominique"; Peter, Paul and Mary's controversial hit "Puff, the Magic Dragon." Was it really about smoking marijuana?

LITERATURE

The Feminine Mystique by Betty Friedan posed the issue of women changing—and not just diapers.

Mary McCarthy's *The Group* shocked the country with its frank and open discussion of women's sex lives including lesbianism. Her fiction also riled several of her former college friends and acquaintances. It was so good at being bad, no one could put it down.

IN THE NEWS

On June 17, the Supreme Court abolished school prayer.

On August 28, two hundred thousand people marched on Washington D.C., to demand equal rights for blacks. Dr. Martin Luther King, Jr., gave his famous "I have a dream" speech.

On November 22, President John F. Kennedy was shot and killed while riding in an open automobile in Dallas, Texas. His wife was at his side in the motorcade. He was rushed to the Parkland Memorial Hospital where he was pronounced dead. Lee Harvey Oswald, a suspect in the assassination, was killed two days later while being taken from the Dallas police headquarters. Oswald was probably the first man ever to be seen being murdered on national television.

SPORTS

The New York Yankees fell under the spell cast by Dodger pitcher Sandy Koufax who helped sweep the boys in pinstripes to a 4–0 Series loss. Koufax even beat the Yankee star pitcher twice during Series play.

Seems like old times: Sonny Liston knocked out Floyd Patterson again to retain the heavyweight championship.

In golf, master Jack Nicklaus won both the Masters and the PGA.

TELEVISION

It seemed like a month in the country on CBS. The silly "Petticoat Junction" and "The Andy Griffith Show" were near the top in the ratings. But the champ was still Jed and all his kin, those "Beverly Hillbillies."

"My Favorite Martian," about a kindly alien (America certainly likes them), appeared on CBS. It starred Ray Walston as the alien and Bill Bixby as his adopted "nephew." Strange things were happening on the small screen.

FADS AND FASHION

Surfing songs, surfing movies, surfing clothes all took the country in a wave of trendiness.

The Whiskey-a-Go-Go opened in Los Angeles. It was the country's first disco.

1964

THE MOVIES

Dr. Strangelove or: How I Learned to Stop Worrying and Love the Bomb directed by Stanley Kubrick. The world was on the edge of destruction. Paranoia was everywhere. Out of Hollywood came the full-tilt answer to anyone's nightmares: the end of the world happened by accident. Director Kubrick played into the shaky hands of those worried about nuclear war and into the minds of anyone with half a brain. This movie was scary. Peter Sellers played multiple roles. George C. Scott and Sterling Hayden helped to dismantle the plot.

Becket directed by Peter Glenville. Richard Burton and Peter O'Toole, two fine actors if there ever were any, were pitted against each other in this heady royal brew. O'Toole was young Henry II, and Burton was the title character, the king's old friend. Duty, honor, and loyalty were the subjects of this film, a spectacular one in all ways.

A Hard Day's Night directed by Richard Lester. The Beatles weren't only rock stars. They packed movie theatres proving their audiences, no matter how young, would spend money on the Fab Four.

Also Notable: *Hush . . . Hush, Sweet Charlotte,* the conspiratorial *Seven Days in May,* and the Rat Pack's *Robin and the Seven Hoods.*

THE PLAYERS

Sean Connery had been around for nearly a decade but had never really been the big star his talents warranted. When Connery played "Bond, James Bond," he finally found himself in a role that could make him a star, even though it did not tax his talents. Many believe Connery did not play James Bond; he became James Bond and no one dare play the role thereafter.

Peter Sellers was a multitalented man who was given the opportunity to let those talents shine in *Dr. Strangelove*. He was very much like the silent comedians of a long ago age, his face full of expression, his manner slightly "different." He played Inspector Clouseau in the Pink Panther movies with the deft clumsiness only he could muster.

Julie Andrews was a big Broadway musical star. But she wasn't big enough to re-create her role in *My Fair Lady*. That part went to Audrey Hepburn, always a big movie star. Andrews had to be content with her role in *Mary Poppins* as a magical nanny. When Oscar time rolled around, Hepburn wasn't even in the running. However, Andrews won the statuette for her consolation part.

MUSIC

Beatlemania swept across the Atlantic and hit our shores like a tidal wave. George Harrison, John Lennon, Paul McCartney, and Ringo Starr, four young musicians from Liverpool, wrote and sang hit after hit. Their influence on music, clothing, hair length, and eventually thought cannot be underestimated. As a group they were news; individually, their lives kept writers typing overtime. Young girls unloosed their sexual fantasies on the four unlike anything since Elvis. "I Want to Hold Your Hand" was a simple enough expression of affection to send girls into a frenzy. "Twist and Shout" took the old rock standard to a new level. "She Loves You" introduced "Yeah, yeah, yeah" to the vocabulary. It was only the beginning.

Out of Detroit a record label (Motown, short for Motor Town) was started by record mogul Berry Gordy. His string of successful groups peaked with The Supremes, that included Diana Ross, Mary Wilson, and Florence Ballard. Their mix of soul, gospel, and pop made them crossover sensations. In 1964, their biggest record was "Baby Love."

In California, the Beach Boys kept the surf sounds alive with "I Get Around."

LITERATURE

John Cheever, America's foremost short story writer, continued to practice his craft, mostly at the prestigious *New Yorker* magazine. His tales of debauchery among the rich and unsteady kept readers fascinated.

Arthur Miller opened his play *After the Fall* at Lincoln Center in New York. He was the first writer to cash in on the death of Marilyn Monroe by painting a totally unflattering portrait of his former wife. Miller needed a hit.

IN THE NEWS

On May 27, the United States military reported it was sending planes to Laos. Due to President Johnson's overwhelming political clout, the Voting Rights Act of 1964 was enacted on June 29.

On August 7, Congress passed the Gulf of Tonkin resolution allowing for presidential action in Vietnam.

On September 27, the Warren Commission report was released finding that Lee Harvey Oswald had acted alone in the killing of President Kennedy. The findings of the Commission have been suspect since the day of their release.

In November, the Democratic ticket of President Johnson and running mate Senator Hubert H. Humphrey overwhelmingly beat the Republicans, Senator Barry Goldwater and Representative William Miller. Johnson's political consultants had cast Goldwater as a war-mad lunatic. A television ad that ran only once showed a girl plucking a daisy, superimposed was a nuclear bomb being exploded. The impression was made: A vote for Goldwater was a vote for destruction. Johnson's "Great Society" was underway.

SPORTS

Sonny Liston was TKO'd in Miami by young Cassius Clay, who now held the heavyweight title.

Philadelphia Phillie Jim Bunning pitched the first regular season perfect game since 1922.

Cleveland Brown, Jim Brown became the first player to rush for more than ten thousand yards. The guy was unstoppable on the field.

TELEVISION

Dr. Richard Kimball did not kill his wife although he was tried and convicted for the murder. Fate intervened, however, and he was set free to find the one-armed man, whom he saw leaving the scene of the crime. This unlikely premise for a hit television series was actually the hook that kept audiences tuned in week after week. David Janssen was "The Fugitive" and Barry Morse was his relentless pursuer. America watched and watched.

"Gomer Pyle, U.S.M.C." was a down-home spin-off from "The Andy Griffith Show," which starred Jim Nabors. Some found the idea insulting that Gomer was a perennial recruit while real American young men were going to Asia to fight and die. But the general good nature of the show made it a hit.

"Bewitched" was nothing more than a television update of the old movie *I Married a Witch,* but it was consistently funny from the first moment it was on the air—at least for its first few years. Elizabeth Montgomery was the sorceress married to a mere mortal, played by Dick York. Agnes Moorehead was the conniving Endora. If anyone knew how to upstage a scene, it was this wonderful veteran actress.

FADS AND FASHION

The Ford Mustang was introduced to a society hungry for its sporty good looks. Ford President Lee Iacocca had the right idea when he dreamed up this car.

Rudi Gernreich introduced his topless swimsuit. It was an eye-popping idea that American women weren't ready for. American men might have been ready for it, though.

Also Notable: Two spooky shows premiered. "The Addams Family" was derived from Charles Addams's *New Yorker* cartoons, and "The Munsters" was a wacky family of monsters and werewolves. John Astin and Carolyn Jones starred in the former, Fred Gwynne and Yvonne De Carlo headed up the latter.

TEEN IDOLS

On September 15, 1964, "Peyton Place" came to nighttime television. The New England town seething with sex was still the same old story, but the players were new. Mia Farrow, the daughter of director John Farrow and screen actress Maureen O'Sullivan (Jane in many a *Tarzan* flick) and director John Farrow, was a striking beauty with long blond hair and a standoffish attitude. She was teamed with athletic Ryan O'Neal. Their undeniable chemistry was at the heart of the show's success.

1965

THE MOVIES

Doctor Zhivago directed by David Lean. Pasternak's story of the Russian Revolution was brought to the screen by the director whose credits always meant class. Lean cast Omar Sharif as Yuri Zhivago, English Julie Christie as Lara, the doctor's love, and Geraldine Chaplin (Charlie's daughter) as his long-suffering wife. Being so deeply entrenched in the Cold War, this was about the only sight Americans had of Russia.

The Spy Who Came in from the Cold directed by Martin Ritt. The spy business was being taken very seriously. James Bond may have been fun, but the world of espionage was treated very dramatically here. Richard Burton was the weathered and beaten spy. The story was unrelentingly gloomy, just as the Cold War made the world appear.

Cat Ballou directed by Elliot Silverstein. Lee Marvin played a dual role in this comedic Western and went on to win an Oscar. Jane Fonda proved she wasn't just Henry's daughter any more. It tickled the funny bone and made people forget what was happening outside the theatre.

Also Notable: the Beatles in *Help!*, *What's New, Pussycat?*, *The Flight of the Phoenix,* and the vastly popular *The Sound of Music,* which was chosen as Best Picture.

THE PLAYERS

Julie Christie had a doubly big year with both *Doctor Zhivago* and her Oscar-winning performance as a British "bird" in *Darling*. She was the epitome of "mod" and "swinging," looks that the English sent over to their American cousins.

Jane Fonda made the family name even more bankable with *Cat Ballou*, a hugely successful comedy. She was a celebrity on her own now.

Rod Steiger had been in films for years but in 1965 he got the public's attention as never before. His brilliant performance in *The Pawnbroker* landed him an Oscar nomination while he received good notices for being so bad in *Doctor Zhivago*.

MUSIC

The Rolling Stones got plenty of "Satisfaction" as their wave of popularity was on the rise in the States.

Seemed like "Yesterday" that the Beatles were at the top of the record charts.

The British Invasion of the mid-60s was obvious by all the English groups on the pop music charts. Herman's Hermits checked in with "Mrs. Brown, You've Got a Lovely Daughter."

Also Notable: Sonny and Cher's "I Got You Babe," and The Supremes' hits "I Hear a Symphony" and "Back in My Arms Again."

LITERATURE

Arthur Hailey's sprawling multistoried *Hotel* was the big, big book of the year. Shallow in substance, the interlocking stories made it feel as if there was more than one book for the price.

Ralph Nader's *Unsafe at Any Speed* was a stinging indictment of the American auto industry. People all over the country hopped in their cars to go buy this book.

IN THE NEWS

On February 21, assassins gunned down the controversial civil rights leader Malcolm X.

Also in February, President Johnson ordered North Vietnam to be bombed below the twentieth parallel.

On August 5, the Voting Right Act was signed by the president.

Between August 11 and 16, the Watts riots in Los Angeles erupt. Thirty-five people were left dead and property damage was estimated at $200 million.

New York saw black. The Big Blackout of 1965 happened on November 9, and hurled millions into darkness.

By year's end American troop strength in Vietnam reached 184,300.

Xerox, the office machine copier, was emerging as big business.

The president promised to wage a war on poverty.

SPORTS

Dodger pitcher Sandy Koufax went 26–8 with eight shutouts and a 2.04 ERA. He led his team to victory over the Minnesota Twins in the World Series.

Muhammad Ali beat both Sonny Liston and Floyd Patterson to keep the heavyweight title his own.

Pete Havlicek stole the ball . . . and he stole the seventh game of the Eastern Division final. The Boston Celtics won the series over the Flyers and went on to victory for the NBA title.

TELEVISION

"Get Smart" was yet another spy-related amusement. The misadventures of Maxwell Smart and Agent 99 were the comic invention of Mel Brooks. The deadpan humor mixed brilliantly with the absurd props and gags. Don Adams and Barbara Feldon worked perfectly smoothly together. "Isn't that right, Chief?"

"Green Acres" with Eddie Albert and Eva Gabor was nothing more than an updated *The Egg and I,* but that was funny, too.

Also Notable: "I Dream of Jeannie" and the offensive, to many, prisoner of war comedy, "Hogan's Heroes."

FADS AND FASHION

Doe-eyed Jean Shrimpton was the world's most recognizable model. Her "mod" clothes and eye makeup were copied by millions.

The Pop art world was dominated by Jasper Johns, Roy Lichtenstein, and Andy Warhol. Their art was "fun" and accessible. Their prices were not.

Lava lamps were unlike anything in home furnishings. It was designed to be hip and cool. It created a mood. Stoned college students could stare at the "lava" blob for hours and consider the world.

The Superball bounced into American homes.

Skateboards knicked knees but were a necessary item for America's youth.

1966

THE MOVIES

The Russians are Coming, the Russians are Coming directed by Norman Jewison. A New England resort community was terrorized by something odd out there in the water. Fear was everywhere. Taken from material by Nathaniel Benchley, director Jewison turned the Cold War and the Russian scare on its ear. He made a comedy of the Soviets invading us. The cast boasted Carl Reiner, Eva Marie Saint, and John Phillip Law. Alan Arkin was the submarine captain who sent the Americans into the jaws of panic.

Who's Afraid of Virginia Woolf? directed by Mike Nichols. Edward Albee's brilliant play was brought to the screen with all its neuroses intact. Were George and Martha substitutes for the Washingtons? Was their child really the United States? Elizabeth Taylor gained weight for the role and gained stature as a serious actress. Richard Burton was her equally pathetic husband. George Segal and Sandy Dennis were the guests invited to a dinner from Hell. This was one of the most verbally brutal movies ever made. Taylor and Dennis were Oscar's ladies of 1966.

Fantastic Voyage directed by Richard Fleischer. It worked for the center of the earth; it could work for the human body. Scientists were shrunk so that they could travel inside a brain. The special effects were terrific and the action was fast moving. Stephen Boyd and Raquel Welch were the intrepid explorers.

Also Notable: *The Sand Pebbles* starring Steve McQueen and *The Fortune Cookie* with Jack Lemmon and Walter Matthau.

THE PLAYERS

Raquel Welch's career was bursting out all over. Her poster was on dormitory walls. Her acting was (in)visible in *Fantastic Voyage.* She was the sex symbol for the moment, a cross between Marilyn Monroe and Victor Mature.

Steve McQueen beat the odds. Few television actors had success-fully crossed over to movie stardom. McQueen was an exception. His quiet brooding made him a latter-day Brando without the angst. He was a star after *The Sand Pebbles,* undeniably.

Elizabeth Taylor and Richard Burton never needed more press at-tention, but that's what they got when they filmed *Who's Afraid of Virginia Woolf?* They did themselves proud and only received good notices. Taylor won her second Oscar.

MUSIC

"The Sounds of Silence" by Simon and Garfunkel was intelligent, quiet rock music. It was also an anthem for the time. The two young New Yorkers carved an unusual path in music: They had lyrics that meant something and a sound that was unforgettable.

From the West Coast came the Mamas and the Papas, a foursome with a melodic sound that captured the easygoing spirit of the beach, much like the Beach Boys with bite. Their hit was "Monday, Monday," and it was a hit for weeks.

Percy Sledge's deep voice made "When a Man Loves a Woman" even more meaningful. He sang like he meant it.

On August 5, John Lennon announced that the Beatles were "more popular than Jesus." Critics crucified Lennon.

Also Notable: The Sinatras, Nancy and Frank. For a few seconds Nancy was a bigger star than her father with her campy hit "These Boots Are Made for Walkin'." Dad sang "Strangers in the Night," his first number one hit. The Byrds sang "Turn! Turn! Turn!"; Donovan's "Sunshine Super-man" sparkled; the pro-war "Ballad of the Green Berets."

LITERATURE

Truman Capote's *In Cold Blood* was something entirely different in American letters. Capote had interviewed hundreds of people over the course of years. The result was not a novel and not journalism. The story of murders in a small Kansas town was shocking.

IN THE NEWS

The Miranda Decision went into effect, requiring police officers to tell a criminal what his/her rights are.

With the world in the shape it was, *Time* ran a cover story, "Is God Dead?" Many people were ready to say yes.

On July 18, race riots broke out in Cleveland, Ohio.

On July 29, Bob Dylan suffered injuries due to a motorcycle accident.

On July 28, and 29, Baltimore, Maryland, was the scene of riots.

On August 1, mental defective Charles Whitman killed fourteen people from a belltower in Texas.

On August 6, Luci Baines Johnson married in the Rose Garden of the White House.

In November, former Warner Brothers star Ronald Reagan became California's governor.

December 2 was the first Friday Catholics could eat meat.

DRUGS

Professor Timothy Leary proclaimed that LSD, lysergic acid, was the sacrament of his new religion.

SPORTS

Jim Ryun was only nineteen years old when on May 13 he ran two miles in only 8:25.2, the third fastest time ever. Then on June 10 he set a world record at 1:44.2 for the half mile. Only weeks later he ran the mile in 3:51.3.

Notre Dame football coach Ara Parseghian was roundly criticized for allowing the clock to run out on a tied game.

Baltimore Oriole Frank Robinson won the Triple Crown and led his team to overtake the Dodgers in the World Series.

TELEVISION

So popular was the camp comedy "Batman" that ABC scheduled it for two nights a week. Adam West and Burt Ward played the caped crusaders, and half of Hollywood made cameos as villains. Vincent Price, Zsa Zsa Gabor, and Burgess Meredith were just a few. The eye-popping graphics and silly expressions—"Holy Swiss Cheese, Batman,"—set this show on a high crest of popularity.

The world premiere on NBC of "Star Trek" on September 8 was not marked by huge hype. However it only took a few shorts weeks to see that this show would have a loyal following. Loyal may not be the word. Devoted was closer. It has become an institution. Captain Kirk, Mr. Spock, and the rest are as much a part of America as Mount Rushmore, and only slightly more animated since they were played with such seriousness by William Shatner and Leonard Nimoy.

FADS AND FASHION

In a world of disposable items, it was only a matter of time before someone introduced the paper dress. Wear it once, throw it away. It didn't catch fire.

Black lights gave the LSD experience another dimension. Now you could take a trip and have the proper atmosphere. Headshops were set up for this and other drug-related paraphernalia.

1967

THE MOVIES

Bonnie and Clyde directed by Arthur Penn. What could have been just another shoot-em-up became a parable about violence in America. In the 1930s the real Bonnie Parker and Clyde Barrow robbed banks and murdered people, but they were nowhere near as attractive as Warren Beatty and Faye Dunaway. With guns going off outside theatres everywhere, audiences somehow felt safe inside where the blood was spilled in beautiful slow-motion. The movie was more than entertainment; it was a sensation.

The Graduate directed by Mike Nichols. An older woman seduced a much younger man. Some saw this also as a parable: the establishment overtaking youth's ambitions. There were many readings to this multilayered tale. All of them thought-provoking. Dustin Hoffman, Anne Bancroft, and Katharine Ross led the cast.

Guess Who's Coming to Dinner directed by Stanley Kramer. The do-gooder liberals (Spencer Tracy and Katharine Hepburn) had their beliefs shaken when their daughter comes home engaged to a black man. Will the parents, both black and white, accept this "new" arrangement? Will America pay to see it on the screen? Maybe it was the star magnetism of Tracy and Hepburn, everyone's unofficial star parents, that made audiences flock in. Hepburn won her second Oscar, twenty-five years after the first.

Also Notable: *In the Heat of the Night* ignited by Rod Steiger and

Sidney Poitier. Steiger and the flick won Oscars; *To Sir With Love* generated by Poitier again; *Valley of the Dolls,* genuinely wonderful trash, and genuinely frightening *In Cold Blood.*

THE PLAYERS

Warren Beatty and Faye Dunaway were no longer only movie stars after *Bonnie and Clyde.* They were certifiable superstars. With their swaggering ways, big, beautiful smiles, and great clothes, they were hot.

Anne Bancroft, Dustin Hoffman, and Katharine Ross in *The Graduate* were responsible for one of the year's biggest critical successes. Bancroft, having been around for years, firmed up her success, while Hoffman and Ross were only beginners now at the zenith.

Spencer Tracy, Katharine Hepburn, and Sidney Poitier made *Guess Who's Coming to Dinner* the hit it was. Of course, Poitier had to embody the perfect black man in too many of his films, but his easy charm meshed with Tracy and Hepburn who had charm to spare. Tracy died soon after the completion of this film; Hepburn won an Oscar for it.

MUSIC

Everyone wanted to know the secret of "Ode to Billie Joe," but singer Bobbie Gentry wisely allowed everyone to come to their own conclusions.

"R-E-S-P-E-C-T" was what Aretha Franklin received from her fans all over America.

Jim Morrison and the Doors knew how to heat things up. Their "Light My Fire" sizzled to the top.

Also Notable: Lulu's "To Sir With Love," from the movie; the Rolling Stones sang a censored version of "Let's Spend the Night

Together" on Ed Sullivan's show; Medieval imagery was borrowed in "Whiter Shade of Pale"; the Beatles' LP *Sgt. Pepper's Lonely Hearts Club Band"* goes to the top.

The Monterey Pop Festival brought together some of the hottest groups.

LITERATURE

Ira Levin's *Rosemary's Baby* was about the devil being born in New York City. Most people believed Satan had been there for years. This was a nail-biting good read.

IN THE NEWS

Smog was not only a noticeable problem in Los Angeles, it was now a health issue.

Interracial marriages weren't just something for Hollywood. A markedly larger number of mixed marriages were being recorded.

On January 3, Lee Harvey Oswald's killer Jack Ruby died in Dallas.

In March it was reported that the use of LSD could lead to genetic damage.

On July 24, forty-three died in the Detroit riots.

President Johnson's daughter Lynda Bird married marine Charles Robb.

On October 21-22 antiwar demonstrators storm the Pentagon.

By December 475,000 American troops were in Vietnam.

DRUGS

Marijuana or "pot" was one of the fastest growing cigarettes in the country.

People experimented smoking dried banana peels.

SPORTS

The first Super Bowl was played on January 15; Green Bay defeated Kansas City, 35–10.

Gordie Howe was the first hockey player to score more than seven hundred goals.

Boston Red Sock Carl Yastrzemski hit forty-four homers, had 121 RBIs and batted .326. In the World Series, though, the Sox lost to the Cardinals, Yaz's average was .400.

Muhammad Ali refused to register for the draft and was stripped of his heavyweight title by the World Boxing Association.

Billie Jean King won both the U.S. Open at Forest Hills and Wimbledon.

TELEVISION

CBS continued to dominate the ratings with its down-home programming.

A new addition to the CBS lineup was "Family Affair" with Brian Keith and Sebastian Cabot. As so often was the case, a single parent family was a happy family. Keith played Uncle Bill to three very polite young children.

FADS AND FASHION

Thin-as-a-rail Twiggy was the rage on both sides of the Atlantic. The only curves on Twiggy were her eyelashes.

Bonnie and Clyde ushered in a retro-look. Everything old was new again. Who would have predicted poverty wear of the 1930s would be a trend in the very trendy 1960s?

"Flower power" was more than just an attitude of the young. It wasn't only the philosophy of "Make Love, Not War." Bell-bottoms, hip-huggers, and very long hair on both males and females abounded.

1968

THE MOVIES

The Lion in Winter directed by Anthony Harvey. Peter O'Toole reprised his King Henry II to costar opposite Katharine Hepburn as Eleanor of Aquitaine. Henry was older but no wiser. Eleanor was just like Hepburn, feisty. The verbal sparring was a delight to the ear; the sets seemed to be early-English. The movie was a feast.

Rosemary's Baby directed by Roman Polanski. Mia Farrow, bird-like, was chosen to be the devil's mother. Shot at Manhattan's famed Dakota apartments, the film suggested gore without showing it. Director Polanski worked well with John Cassavetes and veteran Ruth Gordon, who won an Oscar.

The Producers directed by Mel Brooks. Comic genius Brooks's first featured film was a hip, savvy, and audacious riff on a corrupt Broadway producer. The movie was a howl. Zero Mostel and Gene Wilder pulled out all the stops. The "Springtime for Hitler" number was one of film's most offensive and funny segments.

Also Notable: Barbra Streisand's film debut in *Funny Girl, Romeo and Juliet,* a real make-out movie; Christopher Jones as a real revolutionary in *Wild in the Streets;* Kubrick's legendary *2001: A Space Odyssey.*

THE PLAYERS

Mia Farrow was involved in a scandal that had a much-older man involved with a younger woman. Mia was the younger woman. The man? Frank Sinatra. Farrow, the daughter of Tarzan's Jane (Maureen O'Sullivan) and film director John Farrow, fell in love with "Old Blue Eyes" while she was starring in television's hit "Peyton Place." After they married, she had to bow out of "The Detective," a film she was to do with her man, due to the relationship breaking up.

Barbra Streisand, that songbird from Brooklyn, hit the screen running. In her first role, that of Fanny Brice in *Funny Girl,* Streisand won an Oscar, albeit a shared award with the immortal Katharine Hepburn, who won for *The Lion in Winter.* Hepburn now had three Oscars on her mantel.

Dean Martin had separated from his comedy partner Jerry Lewis in the 1950s, but Martin hit his stride as Matt Helm in a series of spy spoofs.

MUSIC

The very long "Hey Jude" stayed a long time on the charts. Jude didn't let the Beatles down.

Marvin Gaye heard it right when he "Heard It Through the Grapevine." A big, juicy hit for Marvin.

The Beatles' *White Album* was one of the most influential albums of the year.

"In-a-Gada-da-Vita" by the Iron Butterfly was seventeen minutes of unusual joy.

Also Notable: Simon and Garfunkel's "Mrs. Robinson," an ode to older, more experienced women who live empty, suburban lives;

Herb Alpert's off-key "This Guy's in Love with You" that was made bearable by his sincerity (he also owned the record label, A & M); Jeannie Riley's "Harper Valley P. T. A." which was a kind of "Peyton Place" on vinyl.

LITERATURE

Gore Vidal's *Myra Breckinridge* broke all the rules. Seemingly a simple story of Hollywood bed-hopping, it was much more. It cleverly engineered the reader to reconsider sex roles and behavior. This was not for the kiddies!

IN THE NEWS

In February the U.S.S. *Pueblo* was captured by North Korea.

In March, the law dictated all cars had to be manufactured with seat belts.

On April 4, Reverend Martin Luther King, Jr., was assassinated in Memphis. Riots broke out throughout the country.

In April students at New York's Columbia University stormed the administration building and held it hostage.

Hair! premiered on Broadway on April 29. The long-hairs were everywhere in American culture.

On June 5, Senator Robert F. Kennedy of New York was shot and killed at the Ambassador Hotel in Los Angeles. Just moments before Kennedy had thanked a large audience for his victory in the California presidential primary. His body was flown to New York, and then trained to Arlington National Cemetery.

In August at the Democratic National Convention, riots broke out. Mayor Richard Daley's police arrested the instigators, called the "Chicago Seven." The Youth International Party (YIPPIES) was born.

Senator Hubert Humphrey won the nomination on the Democratic slate. His running mate was Senator Edmund Muskie of Maine.

Former Vice President Richard Nixon was the nominee of the Republican party. His running mate was Maryland Governor Spiro T. (Ted) Agnew.

As peace talks continued in Paris, the Republican slate won the general election in November. The three-way race included Alabama Governor George Wallace.

The Motion Picture Association of America put its ratings into effect. From now on *G, M, R,* and *X* were no longer just letters in the alphabet.

SPORTS

Detroit Tiger pitcher Denny McLain went 31–6 for the season, the first pitcher since 1934 to win more than thirty games.

At the Mexico City Summer Olympics, controversy struck when two of America's medal winners raised their fists in a Black Power salute. Tommie Smith and John Carlos sent politicians and sports fans reeling.

Peggy Fleming gracefully twirled for the gold medal at the Grenoble Olympics, her figure skating performance made her a star.

TELEVISION

On January 22 "Rowan & Martin's Laugh-In" became part of the American scene when it debuted on NBC. Irreverent, topical, and like nothing ever before, "Laugh-In" jolted the public out of their seats. Just as the news had been doing, it was now time for comedy to get aggressive. The two leads were old-time stand-up comics, but their supporting cast were all first-rate sketch artists. They included Lily Tomlin, Goldie Hawn, Judy Carne, Richard Dawson, Arte Johnson, Henry Gibson, and Ruth Buzzi.

"60 Minutes" first began ticking on September 24 and hasn't stopped yet. America was missing this sort of coverage since Edward R. Murrow left the airwaves. It newly defined *hard-hitting*. The reporters have changed over the years, but Mike Wallace and his dog-bite approach to hard topics stands tallest in this august group. This show has annihilated its competition and set a new standard for television reportage. Besides that, it's fun to watch just to see how the guilty can squirm on camera.

FADS AND FASHION

Yves St. Laurent tried out his see-through fashion. It was eye-popping but not very successful. Men loved the idea, but women preferred the cover-up.

They were hip. They were hot. They were in style for about fifteen minutes. They were Nehru jackets.

TEEN IDOLS

When he appeared on "Here Come the Brides" in 1968, Bobby Sherman had already been a singer with a large following. His pleasant voice and appearance matched his easygoing nature. Parents were comfortable with him as a role model for their children. His reign was short, however.

"Shindig" and "Hullabaloo" were rock and roll series that featured performers who appealed to the young. Essentially these were "The Ed Sullivan Show" for teenagers; both lasted only one season.

1969

THE MOVIES

Butch Cassidy and the Sundance Kid directed by George Roy Hill. It was an era of men bonding with men in the movies—buddy movies. No two men seemed to bond more effectively than Paul Newman and Robert Redford. As handsome outlaws these two were all smiles and good nature. Forget about history and the real title characters. This show rode on charm. Likable and fun, it tossed Western convention to the wind.

Midnight Cowboy directed by John Schlesinger. This was the first X-rated movie to win the Oscar, although it was far from being pornographic. It did center around a male hustler who came to New York searching for his fortune. In essence another buddy movie, *Midnight Cowboy* plunged deep inside the dregs of society and emerged a winner. Dustin Hoffman and Jon Voight were the outcasts dwelling on the fringe.

Bob & Carol & Ted & Alice directed by Paul Mazursky. The swinging sixties wouldn't have been the same without this foursome. Wife-swapping was a current event—or at least talked about as one. This dynamic double quartet never really got down to business, but the titillation was good enough to bring in audiences.

Easy Rider directed by Dennis Hopper. If there was one movie that typified the era, it was this low-budget throwaway film. It took off

92

like a sky full of firecrackers. Alienation was the key word. Director Hopper and costar Peter Fonda baffled Hollywood establishment types with this "road" movie with a very downbeat ending. In a small role was a man filling in for Rip Torn. His name was Jack Nicholson.

Also Notable: Another Fonda, Jane in *They Shoot Horses, Don't They?;* Arlo Guthrie's *Alice's Restaurant; The Wild Bunch,* and *Goodbye, Columbus.*

THE PLAYERS

Good looking and seemingly good natured, Robert Redford was finally a star with *Butch Cassidy and the Sundance Kid.* His all-American appearance allowed him to become the leading man in demand.

Elliott Gould and Dyan Cannon had been famous for being married, that is to Barbra Streisand and Cary Grant. With *Bob & Carol & Ted & Alice* they didn't have to worry about getting tables at fine restaurants on their own.

Dustin Hoffman and Jon Voight created the kind of magnetism that Gable and Lombard used to. Hoffman, already big and getting bigger, was the sleazy Ratso Rizzo to Voight's innocent Joe Buck.

MUSIC

Things on Earth weren't looking so good so a trip to the future was well timed. Zager and Evan's had a hit with "In the Year 2525."

The Who's rock opera *Tommy* reached our shores.

Elvis was back and he was "In the Ghetto," topical if nothing else.

Jo-Jo and Loretta were the happily married couple in the Beatles' "Get Back"; it sent them back up the charts.

Led Zeppelin II was that group's big LP; the Beatles had *Abbey Road* and the original cast album of *Hair!* all did big business.

On March 12, Paul McCartney married Linda Eastman. Eight days later, John Lennon married Yoko Ono. Many fans went, "Oh, no!"

Also Notable: Johnny Cash's "A Boy Named Sue," Peter, Paul and Mary's "Leaving on a Jet Plane," and Creedence Clearwater Revival's "Bad Moon Rising."

LITERATURE

Portnoy's Complaint by Philip Roth revealed the anxiety of a young Jewish man's guilt. It detailed masturbation. *Oy vey!*

IN THE NEWS

On June 28 a rebellion of another sort rocked New York. Police invaded a gay bar in Greenwich Village and the patrons fought back. The standoff goes on for days. The bar was called Stonewall.

On July 20, Neil Armstrong is the first human to walk on the moon. He says it "is one small step for man, one giant leap for mankind." Edward "Buzz" Aldrin followed in his footsteps while Michael Collins went around and around the moon alone. America was tuned in to this event and watched live. Reports indicated that serious crime dropped off for the night.

On July 18, Senator Edward M. Kennedy was involved in a car accident in which a young woman died. Her name was Mary Jo Kopechne. She is probably the single person responsible for Ted never reaching the White House on his own.

On August 9, pregnant actress Sharon Tate and several others were brutally slaughtered in a fashionable area of Los Angeles.

On August 11 Leon and Rosemary LaBianca were also found killed. Police investigation led to cult leader Charles Manson and his "family." Manson had planned the murders hoping to bring about a race riot. Mentally deranged Manson used the Beatles' "Helter Skelter" to draw his sick ideas from.

In August, the Woodstock Nation was also born. A rock concert in upstate New York became more than just an assemblage of music stars. Between August 15 and 17, 400,000 jammed onto the rolling hills of farmland and brought about a new philosophy. It may have started out as "Peace, love, and understanding," but it segued into "Sex, drugs, and rock and roll." Parents were worried; kids were stoned or turned-on.

SPORTS

The year began with the New York Jets and their cocky quarterback, Joe Namath, beating the pants off the Baltimore Colts 16–7.

On October 16, the Amazing New York Mets, baseball's biggest jokes, beat the Baltimore Orioles in the World Series. In mid-August the Mets were in third place with 9 1/2 games out. They then won a remarkable thirty-eight out the next forty-nine games.

TELEVISION

But they looked nice enough. Not all the "troublemakers" had long hair and bell-bottoms. "The Smothers Brothers Show" on CBS was as irreverent, as say, "Laugh-In," but the big difference may have been the networks the two shows were on. William Paley's CBS was that man's own fiefdom. What he said went. On April 4, Tom and Dick went.

FADS AND FASHION

While everything else seemed to be at sea, the water bed made its
first entry into the American bedroom.

Woodstock was billed as "Three Days of Peace and Music." The
performers, including Jefferson Airplane, The Who, the Grateful
Dead, one-of-a-kind guitarist Jimi Hendrix, and white soul-diva
Janis Joplin, all sang well enough. It was the audience that got out
of hand. The naked and the nearly dead were all over Jasgur's farm.

THE
1970s

The turbulence of the 1960s spilled over into the next decade. The war in Vietnam was still being waged. Protests at home were still commonplace. On April 30, 1970, American troops advanced into Cambodia. Demonstrations erupted almost immediately. In Ohio at Kent State University, the ROTC building was burned down. The National Guard was brought onto campus to quell the protests. On May 4, the National Guard opened fire on the student demonstrators. Four were dead, nine were injured in Ohio. The decade was off to a bad start.

Hippies were now part of the American fabric and that fabric was now tie-dyed and bell-bottomed. Men's hair was long, reminiscent of the Founding Fathers' coiffures, themselves revolutionaries. What began as Flower Power's antiwar stance now bloomed into a burgeoning Counterculture. The length of someone's hair was a measure of how deeply committed they were to the Counterculture.

New freedoms of expression were everywhere. Women were organizing as a group, demanding, among other things, equal pay for equal work. Women's Lib, short for liberation, was at first laughed at, especially by male comedians on television, who were naturally better paid than their female colleagues. The seriousness of intent behind these activist women was no laughing matter. They meant to change the way men looked at women and how women looked at themselves.

There was a lot to look at in the movies. The Motion Picture Association of America, in an effort to resist federal censorship, imposed a rating system on itself. A new frankness and openness was visible on the screen. Of course, more nudity, that is *female* nudity, was also visible. While there had always been movie stars, with the old code gone, audiences were seeing far more of their favorites than ever before.

The movies made many things more acceptable, none perhaps as great as the influence of drugs. Throughout the country the casual use of drugs was growing. No longer solely the problem of inner cities, drugs could now be found anywhere. White suburbia, as well as any blighted urban area, was equally susceptible to the realities of this new drug culture. What teenagers saw in the movies, they copied in real life. Drugs were a way to escape.

On the night of June 17, 1972, a group of former CIA operatives broke into the Democratic Party headquarters in the Watergate Hotel in Washington, D.C. What was dismissed as a minor burglary brought down the White House of Richard Nixon and sent the nation into emotional chaos. No one dared to think the impossible: the President of the United States would use his good office as a means of carrying out "dirty tricks" on his political enemies. America tuned into the Senate Select Committee hearings day after day. There, on television, the best and the brightest that the country had to offer were telling tales of break-ins, enemy lists, cover-ups, and skullduggery. It seemed like spy fiction.

Bob Woodward and Carl Bernstein, two reporters for the *Washington Post,* unearthed the deceptions at the White House. Their book *All the President's Men* read like spy fiction and was later turned into a movie starring Robert Redford and Dustin Hoffman. The movie, which ended with Gerald Ford pardoning Richard Nixon, has been held partly responsible for Ford's defeat at the hands of little-known former Georgia Governor Jimmy Carter in 1976.

President Ford also faced the humiliation of Chevy Chase's zany caricature of the chief executive on television's vastly irreverent "Saturday Night Live." The show broke new ground in lampooning national figures and sacred cows of all kinds. The brilliant cast included Chase, John Belushi, Jane Curtin, Gilda Radner, and Dan Aykroyd. Maybe Ford's defeat was not directly the result of Chase's send-up, but it was the first time on television that a president would be the butt of low-brow jokes week after week.

While politics dominated polite conversation, something completely different was happening behind closed doors. The sexual revolution was in full swing. Meat rack bars opened and flourished

with their clientele of predatory men and women. Sex, once ver-
boten, was now positioning itself as an indoor sport. Not only were
straight people indulging in their fantasies, but so, too, were gays
and lesbians, recently sprung from their closets. It seemed only
Richard Nixon's Silent Majority kept to themselves.

The disco beat was the background music to this new sport, sex.
The soundtrack to the hit movie *Saturday Night Fever* featured several disco-driven songs that became sensations. The thumping beat,
though tiresome to many, was the anthem for the era of toss-away
sex. If one image of the era is emblematic, it is John Travolta posing in his white polyester suit, darkly sexy and unforgettable, no
matter how synthetic.

Athletes were cashing in. Many professional players thought it
was time that they shared in the high profits that team owners were
reaping. With the introduction of free agentry into the high-stakes
game of pro sports, the star athlete was now also a businessman
who took himself seriously as a product. As with any product, the
athlete/businessman had to be merchandised and protected. Some
of the innocence of sports melted away as cost factors dominated
the scene. Young fans no longer merely kept track of a star's RBI
record, but also of his annual salary. And it was the fan who was
hurt the most since the price of admission wasn't just pocket
change.

In 1976 the nation celebrated its bicentennial, renewing itself
with a new president, a man who at first seemed simple and direct
but who was, in fact, much more complicated. However, American
hostages taken in Iran offered the president more complications
than he could handle. President Carter struggled to find a place for
himself, just as the rest of America struggled to find a safe haven
from the storm that was the decade of the 1970s.

1970

THE MOVIES

M*A*S*H directed by Robert Altman. It was a time of irreverence. It was a time to poke fun at war. It was the perfect time for this S*M*A*S*H. The war was Korea, but the message was timeless: war was bloody, lethal, and pointless. The perfect cast was assembled to bring this anti-establishment film to life: Elliott Gould, Donald Sutherland, Robert Duvall, Sally Kellerman, and Jo Ann Pflug. Extremely bloody and extremely funny.

Five Easy Pieces directed by Bob Rafelson. Many thought the title referred derisively to the women in the life of the character Jack Nicholson played. Actually he had hopes of being a concert pianist. Still, the confusion didn't hurt at the box office and demonstrated just how far the censors allowed things to go. The story of desperate alienation was a common one, but it was brought off memorably and depressingly. A rootless man, Nicholson's Bobby Dupea was the ultimate drop-out, having left his family, his jobs, his hopes behind him. The bleak nature of this film perfectly counterpointed the darkness in so many lives at the time. Karen Black, Susan Anspach, and Fannie Flagg were some of the women he encountered.

Little Big Man directed by Arthur Penn. Everything in American society was changing, so why not the way Hollywood looked at Westerns. While *Butch Cassidy and the Sundance Kid* may have been a buddy movie, or even a chase movie on horseback, *Little*

Big Man just turned the idea of good guys and bad guys upside down. It was happening throughout the culture; now it was happening at a movie theatre near you. Dustin Hoffman portrayed a 121-year-old survivor of the Little Big Horn, and Faye Dunaway was a Christian woman with more than salvation on her mind. Richard Mulligan was the doomed George Armstrong Custer.

Also Notable: Frank Perry's poignant *Diary of a Mad Housewife,* and the noxious *Love Story.*

THE PLAYERS

Ali MacGraw and Ryan O'Neal were the stars of the soapy, trashy hit *Love Story.* They were young and beautiful, and in the movie MacGraw died. MacGraw had been a successful model, and O'Neal starred in television's "Peyton Place." Together they had audiences in tears.

The star of *Five Easy Pieces* had kicked around Hollywood for a long time. Suddenly he was a hot commodity. Like only a few things in actual space, he didn't cool off. He was the New Jersey kid, Jack Nicholson, now one of the biggest stars in Hollywood.

Carrie Snodgress starred as the ill-fated Tina Balser in *Diary of a Mad Housewife,* a title that gave away the plot. She was lucky enough to have starred in a film that was on the cutting edge for so many of her fellow women. Housewives were not Donna Reed any more . . . as if they ever were.

MUSIC

It was the sentiment the country needed. Simon and Garfunkel sang about a "Bridge over Troubled Water" and had a mega-hit with both the single and the LP of the same name.

The Temptations were singing about the way things were, too. "Ball of Confusion" matched the mood of the nation.

John Lennon had a hit all on his own: "Instant Karma/We All Shine On."

Also Notable: Led Zeppelin's "Whole Lotta' Love"; Diana Ross and the Supremes' final hit as a group, "Someday We'll Be Together" (but don't bet on it); the Jackson Five's "I Want You Back"; and Miss Ross's first solo "Ain't No Mountain High Enough."

LITERATURE

Jonathan Livingston Seagull by Richard Bach proved to many that the world was for the birds. This inspirational tome featured, yes, a sea gull as the protagonist.

IN THE NEWS

On February 18, a federal jury found the "Chicago Seven" innocent of conspiring to incite riots during the 1968 Democratic Convention. However, five were convicted of crossing state lines to incite riot.

On April 22, the first Earth Day was celebrated with anti-pollution demonstrations.

On May 4, four student demonstrators were killed by the National Guard at Kent State University in Ohio. They were protesting needless murder in Southeast Asia.

The abortion issue was being raised from town to town, city to city.

The economic news was bad: runaway inflation was teamed with a recession.

DRUGS

On September 18, Jimi Hendrix, age twenty-eight, died of a combination of drugs and choking on his own vomit. He died in London.

On October 3, Janis Joplin, age twenty-seven, died of a combination of drugs and booze. She died in Los Angeles at the Landmark Motor Hotel.

SPORTS

Former Yankee pitcher Jim Bouton stunned the sports world with his revealing book *Ball Four.* No one wanted to believe the stories he told were true. The heroics of baseball were fast fading.

Detroit pitcher Denny McLain was suspended for gambling. Two years earlier he had reached his peak by winning thirty-one games.

The Kansas City Chiefs trounced the Minnesota Vikings in the Super Bowl 23–7.

The Baltimore Orioles quickly snuffed the hopes of the Cincinnati Reds in winning the World Series. The Orioles won in five games.

A hero to many, Vince Lombardi, football's legendary coach, died at the age of fifty-seven.

The New York Knicks were the NBA champs for the first time in twenty-four years.

TELEVISION

Robert Young was the star of "Father Knows Best." He returned to the small screen in the avuncular role of "Marcus Welby, M.D." His youthful, motorcycle-riding assistant was played by James Brolin. The medical show was issue-oriented and had a large following.

"The Flip Wilson Show" featured the black comedian in sketch routines and surrounded by guest stars, usually singers. Wilson's "Geraldine Jones" caught on. Like Milton Berle years before, America liked their comedians in drag.

He was a hit when he was the upstanding "Perry Mason," and he was a hit as wheelchair-bound "Ironside." The country loved Raymond Burr.

Everybody loved Lucy. And she was back again. This time, "Here's Lucy" costarred her Arnaz children. They captured the ratings, but they were no Ricardos.

FADS AND FASHION

Writer Tom Wolfe coined the term "radical chic" to describe left-thinking do-gooders who partied with such characters as members of the Black Panthers. Such do-gooders included Leonard Bernstein and his friends.

What do you wear to Earth Day? Well, Earth Shoes, of course. Supposedly it helped you to walk more the way nature intended. Or maybe it just helped the manufacturer.

Hot pants and micro-minis were eyefuls. Some people thought they were awful.

TEEN IDOLS

When "The Partridge Family" debuted in 1970, a lot of ink was spilled over the fact that Shirley Jones was playing the TV mom to her own stepson David Cassidy. The show had one of the sillier premises for a sitcom: a single mother and her brood are part of a rock band. David's androgynous form and pleasant singing voice put him over the top with young girls everywhere.

1971

THE MOVIES

Dirty Harry directed by Don Siegel. The violence in the streets was just too much for some people who felt that one strong cop with the appropriate weaponry could stop it all. The fantasy cop was none other than Harry Callahan, "the San Francisco treat" for law-and-order. Squinty-eyed Clint Eastwood, known for his right-wing politics, was the perfect incarnation of this vigilante policeman. From here on in, Clint was noboby's plate of pasta.

A Clockwork Orange directed by Stanley Kubrick. Set in the bleak future, this movie showed a society devoid of humanity, street gangs running wild, and violence as a part of daily life. When was this again? Malcolm McDowell was the loathsome hero in this allegory from the novel by Anthony Burgess.

The Last Picture Show directed by Peter Bogdanovich. The bleak and desolate Texas of the 1950s was depicted with loving care by director Bogdanovich. The world was a lonely place. It was a black and white place. The movie, shot in black and white, touched a nerve in the public who craved a good story of lost love and redemption. The cast was top-notch: Timothy Bottoms, Jeff Bridges, Cybill Shepherd, Cloris Leachman, Ben Johnson, and Ellen Burstyn.

Also Notable: *The Summer of '42* with Jennifer O'Neill as Dorothy; *The French Connection* which put Gene Hackman on the

Oscar map; *McCabe and Mrs. Miller* with Julie Christie and Warren Beatty, *Klute* with Jane Fonda (winning her first Oscar); the brilliant *Carnal Knowledge* with Jack Nicholson and Ann-Margret; *Harold and Maude,* the cult classic. The old code was gone and new boundaries were being explored. Some of the best Hollywood films were released during this era.

THE PLAYERS

Ann-Margret cast off her sex kitten image to play a sex kitten, albeit an aging kitty. Following the Liz Taylor *Virginia Woolf* strategy, she gained weight and stature among the acting community. She earned an Oscar nomination and more press attention than ever before.

The cast of *The Last Picture Show* was a mixed bag. Some were familiar faces, such as Cloris Leachman, who appeared weekly on "The Mary Tyler Moore Show." Others, like Timothy Bottoms, Jeff Bridges and Cybill Shepherd, were new but dazzling. Shepherd had the edge, however, having been romantically linked to the film's director Bogdanovich.

Like Ann-Margret, Clint Eastwood was finding new success. While no one accused him of acting in *Dirty Harry,* he became a symbol through the part he played. And he became a star. It didn't hurt that he also directed a good first film the same year, *Play Misty for Me.*

George C. Scott didn't like playing in all the reindeer games. He said he was not interested in competing with other actors for honors. When he turned down the 1970 Oscar for *Patton,* he was the first to do so. Hollywood hoped he was the last. Like so many traditions and conventions, no one could even count on the Oscars for pure entertainment any longer.

MUSIC

She was dead but she was still hot. Janis Joplin had a posthumous hit with "Me and Bobby Magee."

Folk rock star Joan Baez got popular attention with her "The Night They Drove Old Dixie Down."

Marvin Gaye had an ecologically aware hit, "Mercy, Mercy Me."

Also Notable: "The Theme from Shaft" by Isaac Hayes won the Oscar for best song; *Tapestry* by Carole King was a soft-as-silk album that stayed and stayed on the charts; Janis Joplin's LP *Pearl,* made her a dead pop heroine.

LITERATURE

Ms. magazine debuted. This was about women on the go—and not pushing carriages. The whole idea of women in America was a different story—coming at you each month.

IN THE NEWS

On January 26, madman Charles Manson and three members of his "family" were found guilty of first degree murder in the Tate/La-Bianca killings in Los Angeles.

On March 10: If you were old enough to go and die for your country, at least now you could vote for the politicians who were sending you there. The U. S. Senate lowered the voting age from twenty-one to eighteen. The Senate vote was 94-0.

On March 29, Lieutenant William L. Calley, Jr., was convicted of premeditated murder in connection with the My Lai Massacre. His life sentence was reduced to twenty years.

At year's end troop strength in Vietnam was down to 140,000.

DRUGS

Jim Morrison, the lead singer of the Doors and sex object for an entire generation of young women, died in Paris on July 3. His drug-related death was instantly a matter of doubt.

SPORTS

In horse racing, the Venezuelan-bred Canonero II almost made it to the Triple Crown, but luck faltered at Belmont.

The Baltimore Orioles had a great year, and they made it last long. In a seven game Series, Baltimore fell to Pittsburgh. At least the fans were happy. It was the first Series to feature a night game.

Muhammad Ali thought of himself as the Dancing Master. But it was no duet with Joe Frazier who knocked Ali for a loop and won the championship by a unanimous decision.

Willie Mays was truly amazing. The San Francisco Giant connected with his three thousandth hit.

TELEVISION

On January 12 television changed forever. Archie Bunker moved onto the block and with him came the kind of language and bigotry that the home screen had never heard. In fact, many people were offended by the racist, sexist, and foolish comments made by Bunker. Producer Norman Lear lapped it up. It was his idea to create a character as a flashpoint for what America was really all about. But were we really about such prejudice? Apparently a nerve was touched which proved that in our homes, behind closed doors, more of us were like Archie than not. There was humor in that. And quite a lot of nervous laughter, to boot. The cast, headed by the talented Carroll O'Connor, was first-rate; it was hard for the country to imagine the actors playing anyone else. Jean Stapleton, Sally Struthers, and Rob Reiner, along with O'Connor brought us

"Meathead," "dingbat," and nearly every racial and ethnic slur imaginable. This was comedy . . . circa 1971.

Also Notable: The mixed religion marriage of "Bridget Loves Bernie," and "Hawaii Five-0," yet another cop show set in the fiftieth state.

FADS AND FASHION

Jesus Christ Superstar! won over Broadway audiences, but offended the tender few who felt it was sacrilegious.

What was EST? Werner Erhard's idea for man transforming himself into the perfect person was nothing new, it just had different initials.

Transcendental meditation was called TM. More initials. In fact, the decade was totally wrapped up in the ME decade, just as writer Tom Wolfe had forecast.

1972

THE MOVIES

Cabaret directed by Bob Fosse. First there was Christopher Isherwood's *Berlin Stories* which were made into the Broadway show *I Am A Camera*. That, in turn, was musicalized for the stage. Then Bob Fosse got his talented hands and feet on the material and transformed it into perfection. The decadent Berlin portrayed here was fast giving way to the ugliness of Nazism, but all the disturbed liveliness was present: Liza Minnelli's sordid Sally Bowles, Joel Grey's wicked emcee, and Michael York's placid bisexual. The music was wonderful . . . and even the band was beautiful.

The Godfather directed by Francis Ford Coppola. Close your eyes for a moment and imagine what we'd be like without this movie. What *Gone with the Wind* was to its generation, so was *The Godfather* to this one. It certainly could have been just another gangster picture, but the impeccable direction, costumes, and acting made it tower over the contenders. Brando returned to being a star, and a cast of young unknowns was discovered overnight. "I made him an offer he couldn't refuse," has become a part of the idiom, as has so much of the visual part of this movie. *The Godfather* was 1972s Oscar pick for Best Picture.

Deliverance directed by John Boorman. Take four urban men and send them down a river in canoes and see what happens. This wasn't merely an adventure movie. This movie showed how fragile human life can be and how cruel human nature certainly is. It was marked by

113

terrific, brawny performances by Burt Reynolds, Jon Voight, and Ned Beatty. "Squeal like a pig" wasn't a line from some kiddie cartoon.

THE PLAYERS

God bless the child who has its own: entertainer Lisa Minnelli won an Oscar for her brilliant performance in *Cabaret*. Both her parents had won also. Her mother (Judy Garland) was given a special statuette as best juvenile lead in *The Wizard of Oz;* her father Vincente Minnelli won the best director award for *Gigi*.

"God bless the child who has its own," was the lyric Diana Ross sang as legendary Billie Holliday in *Lady Sings the Blues*. Ross turned in a great screen performance to show everybody just how supreme she was.

The cast of *The Godfather:* Al Pacino, Robert Duvall, James Caan, Talia Shire and Diane Keaton. These young performers elevated this movie, and they were all comfortable alongside Brando. Brando won his second Oscar and sent Princess Sacheen Littlefeather to refuse the award.

MUSIC

The history of rock and roll was on Don McLean's mind with his mega-hit "American Pie." It was like a coded message that young people were compelled to crack.

Michael Jackson sang a love song. The song was "Ben." Ben was a rat. A dirty rat. It was a big hit for the littlest Jackson.

The British rock group the Moody Blues offered "Nights in White Satin," and it stayed on the charts for days, weeks, and months.

Also Notable: "Catch Bull at Four" (WHAT?) by Cat Stevens, who later became a Moslem fundamentalist, an unusual second career; Jethro Tull's LP *Thick as a Brick* built up a pile of money.

LITERATURE

Joyce Carol Oates wrote about a disturbingly troubled family in *Them*. Their progress, or lack thereof, came to a dizzying climax during the Detroit riots. Oates, who wrote frankly about racial issues when other serious writers begged off, won the National Book Award and a highly regarded reputation.

IN THE NEWS

On February 21, the great anti-Communist Richard M. Nixon arrived in Peking and "opened" China to the West.

On March 22, the Senate approved an equal rights amendment for women. It was then turned over to the states for ratification.

The war in Vietnam escalated again.

On May 22, Richard M. Nixon became the first president to visit Moscow; an arms agreement was reached.

On June 17, five burglars were arrested for breaking into the Democratic National Headquarters at the Watergate in Washington, D.C.

Democratic presidential nominee George McGovern tapped fellow Senator Thomas Eagleton as his running mate. Eagleton, it was discovered, had had shock treatment. In shock themselves, the Democrats dropped him. Kennedy in-law and political appointee Sargent Shriver stepped into the slot.

In November's general election, Nixon/Agnew trounced McGovern/Shriver in a classic conservative versus liberal face-off.

SPORTS

The Munich Olympics was the site of bloody tragedy when eleven Israeli athletes were brutally murdered by terrorists.

American swimmer Mark Spitz won seven gold medals and plenty of product endorsements back home. His face, body, and medals were on display in his popular poster.

The Cincinnati Reds went down to defeat at the hands of the Oakland A's in a seven-game World Series.

In tennis Billie Jean King won the Triple Crown.

TELEVISION

"Sanford and Son" starred Redd Foxx, the black and blue stand-up comic. His nastiness was similar to Archie Bunker's; it just reverberated on another network, NBC. His carryings-on were always fun, even when they were rude or just plain lies, like his faked heart failure. "It's the big one, Elizabeth," he'd call to his dead wife.

If it worked in the movies didn't necessarily mean it would work on TV. Many hit movies were revamped for the small screen, but few were successful. The big exception was "M*A*S*H" which starred Alan Alda, Loretta Swit, Wayne Rogers, and Gary Burghoff, adapted from the film version. War had been lambasted before, but never with such glee. America had been waiting for this comic relief from the nightly news shows of what real war could do. The writing was consistently excellent, as was the cast. A bit wobbly at first, due to its canned laughter, which was later ditched. This was pure American comedy.

Also Notable: The quiet show that could (and did)—"The Bob Newhart Show" was a sleeper. Newhart himself was something of a somnambulist who came awake with a wry humor. With "the hams on wry," this show dished up success. The incomparable Suzanne Pleshette purred as doting wife Emily, and Bill Daly was the insecure navigator-neighbor, Howard.

FADS AND FASHION

Liza Minnelli's hair bob had a "short cut" to success.

Eight-track tape players replaced albums as the venue of choice for music lovers.

1973

THE MOVIES

American Graffiti directed by George Lucas. Those sweet and innocent 1950s were back. But were they so sweet and innocent? This patchwork of connecting stories was funny with a strong sense of melancholy running underneath the smiling facade. This retrothinking yanked audiences out of the 1970s where nothing was going right to a time when nothing went wrong. Ron Howard, Suzanne Somers, Harrison Ford, Richard Dreyfuss, and Cindy Williams were perched for fame in this vehicle.

If the streets weren't safe, neither were your dreams after seeing *The Exorcist* directed by William Friedkin. Gruesome, bloody, and very scary, the powerful thing about *The Exorcist* was that it stayed with you. It crept into your dreams. It was a nightmare for audiences who had never really seen a mainstream film so gory before. It was a bonanza for the filmmakers who watched as lines of people circled city blocks. It was enough to put the fear of God back into Hollywood moguls' hearts.

The Way We Were directed by Herbert Ross. This was just the old-fashioned love story "they" said wasn't made any more. In fact, it was a politically tuned love story set against the Blacklisting days of the 1950s—those good old days, if you weren't being hounded by the FBI. Barbra Streisand was hotter than a pistol, as was her costar, Robert Redford.

Also Notable: Jack Nicholson in *The Last Detail;* Marlon Brando with a stick of butter in *Last Tango in Paris,* and lastly *The Paper Chase.*

THE PLAYERS

The biggest male star of the 1950s had taken his hits with his misses and had fallen on bad times. With the previous year's *The Godfather,* it seemed as though the king had returned to his throne. And when *Last Tango in Paris* opened, it was assured that his ascent was true. However, Marlon Brando was never an easy man to figure out. When he rejected his Oscar for *The Godfather* on that spring night in 1973, he was rejecting more than a mere statuette. He was turning his back on the people he had worked with, his own career, and the American public. By sending a bogus Native American Princess Sacheen Littlefeather to speak for him, Brando miscalculated even further.

MUSIC

Rumor had it that Carly Simon was singing about playboy Warren Beatty in her stinging "You're So Vain." What was a fact: Mick Jagger sang back-up on the hit single.

Elton John went to the top of the charts with "Goodbye, Yellow Brick Road," the single and the LP.

"Brother Louie" was sung by Stories and was very topical. The story of scorned interracial romance was a story told again and again in real life.

Also Notable: Stevie Wonder had a chart-topper with "You Are the Sunshine of My Life"; Paul McCartney and his new group Wings sang "My Love"; Eric Weissberg had an instrumental hit with "Dueling Banjos," from the film *Deliverance.* Roberta Flack sang "Killing Me Softly with His Song," a tribute to 1972's "Golden Boy" Don McLean.

LITERATURE

When a writer such as Norman Mailer tackled a subject, that subject usually stayed tackled. Not so with the topic of his latest book. *Marilyn* was a fictionalized rethinking of Monroe's life caught in the ribbons of Mailer's typewriter. He was the first to proffer, between hard covers, that her life may not have ended in the manner the authorities put forth. But from this book on, Monroe was no longer merely a dead blonde actress from the 1950s. With the revelation, real or imagined, of her liaisons with the brothers Kennedy, Monroe became an historical character.

IN THE NEWS

In January, five of the seven in the Watergate break-in pleaded guilty. The other two were convicted.

Also in January, the Supreme Court overruled restrictions on abortion laws.

The draft was abolished on January 27. A new lottery system put young men at the mercy of mere numbers.

A "peace-with-honor" had been negotiated in Vietnam. The last American troops left that nation on March 29. The fates of many MIA's were left unaccounted for.

On October 10, Vice President Spiro T. Agnew resigned and pleaded "nolo contendere" to tax evasion charges. Representative Gerald R. Ford was picked by Nixon to become the new vice president replacing the old vice.

On October 20, President Nixon fired Archibald Cox, the Watergate special prosecutor. Attorney General Elliot Richardson resigned rather than fire Cox. William Ruckelshaus, Deputy Attorney General, was also fired for refusing to do the deed. The

hatchet job fell to Solicitor General Robert H. Bork. The incident
was called "The Saturday Night Massacre."

SPORTS

Buffalo Bills running back O. J. Simpson rushed for more than two
thousand yards, breaking an NFL record.

Muhammad Ali had his jaw broken in his April bout with Ken
Norton.

Joe Frazier was knocked out by George Foreman for the heavyweight title.

In what was termed the "Battle of the Sexes," Billie Jean King beat
Bobby Riggs 6–4, 6–3, and 6–3. So much for men being better than
women in tennis.

TELEVISION

Joining the down-home theme on CBS was the Depression-era family, the very upbeat "Waltons." They were poor, simple, country-
people; they were a hit with a public tired of the energy crisis.

Peter Falk, the terrific character actor from dozens of films, came to
television after Bing Crosby passed on the role. The character was
"Colombo," and Falk's career was set forever.

FADS AND FASHION

The skinny little T-shirt or tank top became a fashion staple for
both men and women. Derived from New York's West Village homosexual's clone garb, it was cool at least.

1974

THE MOVIES

Chinatown directed by Roman Polanski. On the surface this was just another detective movie of the old school: hard-bitten and slightly libidinous. But scratch the surface and there was utter corruption, down to the very soul of Los Angeles. Bogart would have been proud to have been near this movie. His old director, John Huston, was in it. As Noah Cross he was evil incarnate. His daughter was played by Faye Dunaway, and she had a stunning, shocking scene where she admits her incestuous past with Cross. As J.J. Gittes, Jack Nicholson towered over everything and everybody, except the ending. In a bleak world, it was argued that a bleak ending was necessary. In fact, the conclusion drives home the despair.

Lenny directed by Bob Fosse. The life story of comic Lenny Bruce was a fierce trip filled with anger and drugs. Dustin Hoffman, again on-target, played the erstwhile stand-up, but nothing could make Bruce lovable. Bruce fought the obscenity laws that landed him in jail and in tubs of hot water within the entertainment world. What he said on stage was nothing compared to what would come after him.

Blazing Saddles directed by Mel Brooks. The height of bad taste, this movie was most famous for its bean-eating scene. If only they had cut away! But funny, funny. And it was just what the doctor ordered in a time of such political and social turmoil. Brooks took the

Western and made it hysterically funny. Unforgettable scenes include Madeline Kahn's seduction of Cleavon Little, her singing "I'm Tired," and, of course, the very famous bean-in-action sequence.

Also Notable: Martin Scorsese's *Alice Doesn't Live Here Anymore;* Francis Ford Coppola's *The Conversation* and Academy Award-Winning *The Godfather Part II;* and *Murder on the Orient Express,* the first of a long line of Agatha Christie-based films. *The Great Gatsby* should be noted, too, for how it bombed with the critics and with audiences; expectations had been very high.

THE PLAYERS

Playing a young Vito Corleone, a little known New York actor stole *The Godfather II* from some very heavy hitters. The young man's name was Robert DeNiro, and he won an Oscar for aping Brando's towering lead.

Valerie Perrine exploded as Lenny Bruce's stripper wife Honey.

Having kicked around show business for years, veteran actor Art Carney finally got the respect he deserved when he won an Oscar for *Harry and Tonto.*

MUSIC

"Cat's in the Cradle" by Harry Chapin was his generation's slap at the previous one caught up in ambition and greed without giving proper time and emphasis on childrearing. Naturally, spoiled and self-centered listeners saw themselves in the situation, and the record was a big hit.

One of the biggest hits of the year was written in 1902 by Scott Joplin. Marvin Hamlisch had a hit with "The Entertainer" from the 1973 Academy Award-Winning movie *The Sting.*

"Tell Me Something Good" was really good for the group Rufus.

Also Notable: "The Bitch is Back" by Elton John, Steely Dan's "Rikki Don't Lose that Number," and "Kung Fu Fighting" by Carl Douglas that led the kung fu craze of the era.

LITERATURE

Jaws by Peter Benchley was one of the biggest selling first novels of all time. Coming from a distinguished writing family could not have hurt Benchley. If the plot of this movie is strikingly similar to *The Russians are Coming, The Russians are Coming;* it could be his father wrote that.

IN THE NEWS

On April 2 during the Academy Awards ceremonies, a streaker dashed across the stage. (Streakers, then all the rage, were people who stripped and ran.) Never losing his cool, dapper David Niven said, "Ladies and gentlemen, that was bound to happen. Just think the only laugh that man will probably ever get is for stripping and showing off his shortcomings."

On a much more serious note: On July 30, the House Judiciary Committee voted to impeach President Richard Nixon.

On August 8, President Nixon resigned. Gerald Ford was sworn in as the thirty-eighth President of the United States.

Gas shortages were still a national issue.

Heiress Patty Hearst was kidnapped by the Symbionese Liberation Army. Hearst was seen on videotape helping her captors rob a bank.

The recession was still with us and so was mounting inflation.

On September 8, President Ford must have heard someone say "Pardon me," because that's what he did for former President Nixon.

SPORTS

It was old hat: The Miami Dolphins won the Super Bowl again, and the Oakland A's with star Reggie Jackson won their third straight World Series.

Bjorn Borg of Sweden became a hot name in men's tennis.

On April 8, Henry "Hank" Aaron swung at a high fastball and connected. The ball soared into the Braves' bullpen. Aaron's record was set: 715 homers.

TELEVISION

"Chico and the Man" starred young comedian Freddie Prinz and veteran Jack Albertson. It was all chemistry, and it worked.

"The Mary Tyler Moore Show," which debuted in 1970 was still going strong. Moore, who had honed her comic skills on the old "Dick Van Dyke Show," was irresistible as Mary Richards, girl news producer turned woman. It was Mary Richards more than nearly any one else, real or fictional, that inspired women to be all that they could be. Single, sharp, and always friendly, both Richards and Moore were great role models. This program also produced many spin-offs: "Rhoda," "Phyllis," and later "Lou Grant." This was unquestionably one of the most important shows of the decade.

"The Carol Burnett Show" debuted on CBS in September 1967. It was part of that network's unbeatable Saturday night lineup that also included "The Mary Tyler Moore Show" and "The Bob Newhart Show." Burnett and her talented supporting cast danced, sang, and acted in some of the funniest skits ever put on videotape. Vicki Lawrence, Harvey Korman, Lyle Waggoner, and Tim Conway were all great. The most memorable creation from the show was the dysfunctional-and-proud-of-it Eunice and her family. It could have been utterly sad if it hadn't been so funny. A very high highlight was the family playing "Sorry." No one was ever sorry.

What *American Graffiti* did for films, "Happy Days" did for television, even going so far as to casting the film's lead, Ron Howard, as the star. It was a throw-back to the good old, happy days of the 1950s when all mothers wore pearls to clean up and all fathers knew best. In a supporting role was Henry Winkler as Arthur Fonzarelli, an incipient hood with slicked back hair and a leather jacket. In the real 1950s this image was not encouraged by thoughtful parents, but in the remade world of television, "The Fonz" was a font of information, intelligence, and clean-cut behavior. Of course he was a real ladies man, to boot. Fonzie's "A-a-ay!" worked its way into the language of the time. Whereas the simple-themed shows of the 1950s were honestly simple-minded, this show lied about the past, about how people behaved, and what was acceptable. It was a big hit.

FADS AND FASHION

Lauren Hutton was supermodel A Numero Uno, closely affiliated with Revlon products.

The Great Gatsby may not have been a good movie, but it did spur a retro look in fashion.

Streaking may have been derided on television, but it was still a very big thing on college campuses, no matter who you were.

TEEN IDOLS

"Starsky and Hutch" was a buddy cop show. With two heartthrobs (David Soul and Paul Michael Glaser) in the title roles, ABC was assured success. Soul had been popular on "Here Come the Brides" and enjoyed a tepid singing career. Glaser later became a director and an AIDS activist after his family became infected with HIV.

1975

THE MOVIES

One Flew Over the Cuckoo's Nest directed by Milos Forman. Jack Nicholson reached a career peak as R. P. McMurphy, the mental patient, who wasn't really crazy, but that didn't stop the powers that be from turning him that way. Nicholson fit this role perfectly. As Nurse Ratched Louise Fletcher got a role no other major actor wanted. For her trouble Fletcher won the Oscar. But then, so did the movie, the director, and Nicholson for a performance that captured his generation on screen.

Shampoo directed by Hal Ashby. Warren Beatty was a Beverly Hills hairdresser with the inside dirt on all his ladies. That was easy since he was sleeping with all of them. *He* was the dirt. This stylish comedy of manners was more than just funny, though. It understood the different levels people interact on, how human nature was a frail thing. Beatty earned plenty of respect for producing this. The cast included Goldie Hawn, Julie Christie, Lee Grant, and a very young Carrie Fisher, in her first film role.

The Rocky Horror Picture Show directed by Jim Sharman. When first released, Twentieth Century Fox was nervous. The plot was delirious. The production was ramshackle. Who knew that this would turn out to be one of the biggest cult classics of all time with late-night shows and audiences actually knowing each and every line? Susan Sarandon, Tim Curry, and Barry Bostwick are the darlings of the midnight movie crowd. There was no accounting for taste, except with the CPAs at Fox.

Also Notable: Sidney Lumet's one-of-a-kind New York bank robbery movie, *Dog Day Afternoon;* Stanley Kubrick's stoic *Barry Lyndon;* Woody Allen's contemplative comedy about *Love and Death.*

THE PLAYERS

Nobody and nothing was hotter than Jack Nicholson. He starred with his good buddy Warren Beatty in *The Fortune* and in Michelangelo Antonioni's *The Passenger.* But Nicholson didn't need to make another film to be remembered forever after he did *One Flew Over the Cuckoo's Nest.* He blew away the competition. As McMurphy he captured the essence of the times, the edginess, the combustibility. The reckless kid from Neptune, New Jersey, was now one of the biggest movie stars.

The large cast of *Nashville* included Ronee Blakely, Keith Carradine, Lily Tomlin, Henry Gibson, and had cameos by Julie Christie and Elliott Gould.

Al Pacino played a real-life New York bank robber who needed the money so that his boyfriend (Chris Sarandon) could get a sex change operation. How many Hollywood stars would play a character like that? Only the risk-taking Pacino.

MUSIC

American music was dominated—again—by foreigners. The theatrical David Bowie, the ever-cha-cha-changing rock star from Britain had a big hit with "Fame."

Another glitter group Queen hit the top of the charts with "Bohemian Rhapsody." No one thought they were named after royalty.

From West Germany came Kraftwerk and the instrumental hit "Autobahn."

A kid from Freehold, New Jersey, Bruce Springsteen made a big impression with his album *Born to Run.*

The writing was on the wall for Led Zeppelin's *Physical Graffiti* to become a hit.

Also Notable: The birth of disco. Dance clubs sprouted up all over the place and what people were dancing to was Van McCoy's "The Hustle." Although many people disparaged the craze, millions bought records such as "Disco Lucy," a revamped version of the "I Love Lucy" theme music. Perhaps this was going too far.

LITERATURE

Looking for Mr. Goodbar by Judith Rossner was loosely based on a real New York story of a young woman brutally slain after picking up a bad trick in a single's bar. It was a tale told too often in the headlines and a cautionary one told for participants of the sexual revolution.

IN THE NEWS

In May, the American freighter *Mayaguez* was captured by a Cambodian torpedo boat. In an effort to rescue the vessel, thirty-eight Americans died.

In June, union leader Jimmy Hoffa disappeared. He was never found, but rumor had it that he was buried on the fifty yard line at Giant Stadium. No one knew Hoffa had been such a big football fan.

Seagram's heir Samuel Bronfman, II, was kidnapped and had his ear cut off by his captors.

There was an attempt on President Ford's life.

The historic headline, "Ford to City: Drop Dead," explained in five short words that the president was unwilling to allow any federal bail-out of financially strapped New York City. His popularity in the Big Apple dropped to a depth below the Hudson River.

Also in New York, *A Chorus Line* opened at the Shubert Theatre. A completely new and exciting theatrical event, staged by Michael Bennett, it was there for a record-setting run.

SPORTS

In a media-crazed fight, Muhammad Ali outboxed opponent Joe Frazier to win the fourteen-round "Thrilla in Manilla." Ali's every punch was reported by Howard Cosell, the much-disliked sportscaster.

The Pittsburgh Steelers beat the Vikings at the Super Bowl.

Jimmy Connors lost Wimbledon to Arthur Ashe. Connors was the first of the tennis "brats."

The Cincinnati Reds beat the Boston Red Sox in dramatic seven game series. Carlton Fisk batted on out during the sixth game to become a big hero.

TELEVISION

"Saturday Night Live" premiered. Twenty-nine-year-old executive producer Lorne Michaels and twenty-eight-year-old NBC executive Dick Ebersol put together a knock-out cast of zanies: Gilda Radner, Jane Curtin, Dan Aykroyd, Chevy Chase, John Belushi, Garrett Morris, and Laraine Newman. More closely related to "Rowan and Martin's Laugh-In," than to the currently running, traditional "Carol Burnett Show," "SNL" broke every rule, every taboo, and every ratings for its 11:30 Saturday night slot. It spawned an entire generation of performers, writers, and films. Directly out of it came the movies *The Blues Brothers, Wayne's World,* and *The Coneheads.* As the years ticked by other performers who hit their first marks included: Eddie Murphy, Billy Crystal, Dana Carvey, Mike Myers, Julia Louis-Dreyfus, and Gilbert Gottfried. Famous for having a guest host each week, those who performed that duty were a virtual "who's who" of show business.

FADS AND FASHION

In a gawky era of platform shoes, polyester suits, and wide collars came other manias: Mood rings, costing as little as $2 and as much as hundreds of dollars swept the nation. They tantalized customers by claiming to know more about the wearer than he or she knew about him/herself. "Tell me more about me."

An inspired bit of pointlessness was the Pet Rock. It was all in the marketing. And P. T. Barnum was ultimately right: You'll never go broke underestimating the taste of the American public. People actually bought painted rocks. Some must have fallen out of their heads.

1976

THE MOVIES

Taxi Driver directed by Martin Scorsese. "You talkin' to me?" asked Travis Bickle of himself. Paranoia, loneliness, desperation, all the things that go into the mind of an assassin were evident in this very violent look at one of the fringe people who was making the news—wayward political killers. Robert DeNiro proved to be someone no one wanted to have dinner with. Jodie Foster as a teenage prostitute had years of experience etched on her face.

Network directed by Sidney Lumet. "I'm mad as hell and I'm not going to take it any more." People on the streets felt the same way. It took screenwriter Paddy Chayefsky to encapsulate the feeling of chaos in an otherwise crazy world. Never had television been skewered quite so demonically. Since society revolved around the television, it only made sense to build a mad world around the business of television. Tabloid shows were encouraged in this movie. In 1976 it seemed too unbelievable for things like that to really get programmed on the tube. William Holden played a weary executive, and Oscar winners Peter Finch and Faye Dunaway gave thrilling performances.

Rocky directed by John G. Avildsen. The underdog went the distance against enormous odds. This was an Everyman story set in the boxing world with relative unknown Sylvester Stallone writing and acting his way to glory. Stallone's own determination to get this movie made sounded just like the plot. The film went on to win big at the box office and won Best Picture at the Academy Awards.

Also Notable: *All the President's Men* may have helped Jimmy Carter become president as it showed President Ford pardoning former President Nixon in the final reel; *Carrie,* based on Stephen King's novel; Alfred Hitchcock's last film *Family Plot;* the disastrous *The Last Tycoon.*

THE PLAYERS

Sylvester Stallone came out of nowhere, just like his movie hero in *Rocky,* and knocked out the competition.

Sissy Spacek, cousin to actor Rip Torn, made a big name for herself as the put-upon teenager in *Carrie.*

Peter Finch won an Oscar months after his death. He was the first actor to be so honored.

MUSIC

Peter Frampton's *Frampton Comes Alive!* was one of the biggest selling albums of all time.

"Fifty Ways to Leave Your Lover" by Paul Simon was a melancholy tune from an album filled with melancholy, *Still Crazy After All These Years.*

Rod Stewart's "Tonight's the Night" featured his girlfriend Britt Ekland in the background singing French jibberish. We knew what he meant.

Also Notable: Stevie Wonder's LP *Songs in the Key of Life.* Disco was still in full swing.

IN THE NEWS

Pornography had people seeing blue.

On July 4, the country celebrated its two hundredth birthday. The gifts were large sailing vessels that arrived from all over the world and met in New York Harbor. That's where the Statue of Liberty could keep an eye on all those sailors.

A new and mysterious disease was discovered when several conventioneers died from it in Philadelphia. It was called Legionnaire's Disease

In the November presidential election, former Georgia Governor James Earl (Jimmy) Carter and his running mate Senator Walter (Fritz) Mondale beat incumbent President Ford and his running mate, hatchet man Kansas Senator Robert Dole.

SPORTS

The sports world was captivated by the Montreal Olympics. A young girl from Communist Romania, Nadia Comaneci won over the hearts of Americans as she won three of a possible five gold medals in gymnastics.

American Bruce Jenner won a world-record decathalon, and he quickly became a marketing promoter of himself.

The big losers in football were Tampa Bay. They lost all fourteen of their games.

TELEVISION

"Charlie's Angels" were young and beautiful girls who worked undercover to ferret out criminals. They wore tight clothes, had gorgeous hair, and skimpy-minded plots. Farrah Fawcett, Kate Jackson, and Jaclyn Smith were what America needed to take their minds off what was really happening to the nation.

"Alice" arrived on August 31. She was once *Alice Doesn't Live Here Anymore,* but CBS must have felt it necessary, in the belt-tightening mode, to trim her title. Alice was still a waitress and still a hit. Alice was now Linda Lavin. Diane Ladd had turned down the role of Flo she had made famous in the film. She soon changed her mind and took another part on the very popular program.

Daytime soaps were always popular with "housewives," but now college campuses were filled with groupies for such shows as "All My Children." Susan Lucci, as that show's vixen, was especially popular.

Lindsay Wagner was "The Bionic Woman," an Adam's rib to "The Six Million Dollar Man."

FADS AND FASHION

Acupuncture was being taken seriously by more and more Americans, even people with such serious conditions as emphysema.

TEEN IDOLS

In 1976 "Charlie's Angels" made Farrah Fawcett a star, but her biggest fame stemmed from her hairdo. Her form and hair were featured in a very popular poster that graced many a young boy's wall. Fawcett, along with Jaclyn Smith and Kate Jackson, played a trio of detectives on "Charlie's Angels." The plots were only devices to show off the three very attractive females.

1977

THE MOVIES

Annie Hall directed by Woody Allen. The director/writer/star's brand of New York humor had made Allen a critical darling for years. Now he had a bona fide hit with this semi-autobiographical study of his life with Diane Keaton, whose real last name was Hall. Just a New York kind of guy, Allen got a lot of mileage out of Southern California jokes, the television business, and love. He also won the Oscar for Best Director and his film, Best Picture.

Saturday Night Fever directed by John Badham. A Brooklyn boy, John Travolta, dreamed of the big time, way over in Manhattan. His roots were strictly outer-borough, however, and so was his lifestyle, which was dancing. He was the king of the dance floor, with very little else to recommend him. Travolta gave the performance of his life as the "diamond in the rough" guy who wanted to do better. If he could only get over that bridge. This was the heyday of disco, and the movie crossed over all kinds of boundaries to be a hit.

Star Wars directed by George Lucas. A whole new way of looking at the movies was hatched because of this film. Space was really *in*. Special effects never mattered so much, and from here on in would matter even more. Harrison Ford, Carrie Fisher, and Mark Hamill fought the forces of evil, complete with the voice of James Earl Jones. "May the Force be with you" temporarily replaced the more mundane "Have a nice day."

Also Notable: *Julia,* the controversial adaptation of Lillian Hellman's memoir; Steven Spielberg's cosmic *Close Encounters of the Third Kind,* the Richard Burton starrer *Equus.*

THE PLAYERS

John Travolta graduated from the high school of "Welcome Back, Kotter" on television to full-blown screen star with his role as Tony Monero in *Saturday Night Fever.* Not only was he popular but so were his polyester clothes.

Jacqueline Bisset did more for the bathing suit in *The Deep* than all the designers in the country. Her poster was a young boy's necessity.

Diane Keaton *was* Annie Hall. But she was also the victim in *Looking for Mr. Goodbar,* the story of a prim schoolteacher who picked up men at singles' bars. Keaton showed she could play both light comedy and heavy drama. She weighed in with an Oscar for *Annie Hall.*

MUSIC

The Eagles scored a big success with their LP *Hotel California,* where check-out time was at the cash register. The title cut proved to be only one of many hits from the disc.

Fleetwood Mac's *Rumours* album climbed the charts and stayed there, becoming one of the top sellers of all time.

The soundtrack to *Saturday Night Fever* heated up the charts with singles such as "How Deep is Your Love?" and "More than a Woman." The people responsible were the Bee Gees, the Australian group of brothers.

Also Notable: "I'm in You" by Peter Frampton; "You Light up My Life" by Debby Boone, the daughter of Mr. White Bread from the 1950s Pat Boone.

LITERATURE

It was the year of Cold War spy novels. John le Carré was the master of the genre.

IN THE NEWS

On January 20, Jimmy Carter was inaugurated president. He promised to restore faith in government. His wife Rosalynn was often criticized for offering too much advice to her husband and for sitting in on cabinet meetings.

On July 13, the Big Blackout of 1977 struck New York City. A thunderstorm upstate struck power lines and led to twenty-five hours of looting and many hours of darkness.

On August 10, David Berkowitz was arrested as the "Son of Sam" killer after terrorizing an already panicky New York. He was notable for wanting to publish his memoirs, but New York State put an end to his plans by enacting laws against criminals benefiting financially from their crimes.

Anita Bryant led a crusade against homosexuals.

On August 16, the King was dead. Elvis Presley died of a combination of drugs, hard living, and an allergic reaction to sequins. The performer had lost his rock and roll image long ago and had become Mr. Las Vegas. His fans would always love Elvis no matter what he did.

SPORTS

Yankee Reggie Jackson slugged his third home run in the sixth and last game of the World Series. New York beat Los Angeles in what looked like a television rerun from years before.

Ted Turner, the millionaire from Georgia, sailed his ship *Courageous* to beat Australia for the America's Cup.

Cale Yarborough won the Daytona 500.

Tom Seaver was traded to the Cincinnati Reds.

TELEVISION

"LaVerne & Shirley," the "Happy Days" spin-off, was a salute to 1960. Starring Penny Marshall and Cindy Williams, the "girls" worked in a brewery and had big dreams of getting out of Milwaukee. Their slapstick approach to comedy was reminiscent of Lucy and Ethel.

"Roots" was a spectacularly successful miniseries that had the great good fortune of being telecast during one of the coldest winters the East had known. Whatever the reasons, though, the show appealed to all viewers, and it set ratings records.

FADS AND FASHION

Annie Hall clothes were definitely in. The look that Diane Keaton had made famous featured intentionally baggy, tailored trousers, hats with brims flipped up, dark and round sunglasses, and men's vests.

The white polyester suit and black open collared shirt worn by John Travolta in *Saturday Night Fever* caught on in a flash at all the hottest discos.

Star Wars kicked off more than just movie ticket sales. All kinds of toys sprang up around Luke Skywalker and his pals. Especially loved were the toys featuring R2D2 and C3P0, the robots from the film. Merchandising of products from films was now an important way for companies—and stars—to make extra money.

TEEN IDOLS

There was talent to spare in the Cassidy family. Shaun was the son of actor Jack Cassidy and his Oscar-winning wife Shirley Jones. He got his time in the sun when "The Hardy Boys" debuted in 1977. His singing career kept him in the limelight for several years longer.

Suzanne Somers had appeared as the mysterious object of desire in *American Graffiti,* but it took "Three's Company" to make Somers a full-fledged star. Her winsome ways and blonde buxomy form made her an easy target for jokes. But her comic timing was impeccable, if largely derived from Judy Holliday and Marilyn Monroe. Somers believed she was as big a star as those two immortals and wanted more money to continue her hit series. The producers balked. She could have written the book, *Why Never to Leave a Hit Series,* instead years later she wrote her own sad story about her alcoholic father.

1978

THE MOVIES

Midnight Express directed by Alan Parker. A young and attractive American, played by Brad Davis, is held in a Turkish jail for a silly little thing like drug smuggling. Based on a real-life story, this movie makes the drug dealer into a hero, thus confusing quite a few people in the audience who always thought drug smugglers were criminals. The movie was most effective in showing the awful conditions in Turkish jails, and the resolution was truly exciting. However, it was movies like this one that got Hollywood into hot water about where it stood on the issue of drugs. The screenplay filled with lies was by Oliver Stone.

Grease directed by Randal Kleiser. Riding the wave of nostalgia for the good old days of the 1950s, this musical was first a long-running Broadway hit. When John Travolta starred as a greaser from the Eisenhower fifties, it looked like everything was set for success. It was. Olivia Newton-John, Stockard Channing, and Jeff Conaway were also cast. Without establishing a clear view of how America currently saw itself, it was easier to look backwards. This hit movie was a result of that looking over our collective shoulder.

The Deer Hunter directed by Michael Cimino and *Coming Home* directed by Hal Ashby were two very different Vietnam war movies and both vied for major awards throughout the year. Oscar-winning *The Deer Hunter* was an elegiac look into the sorry lives of the grunts who went to fight the war and its aftermath; *Coming*

Home politicized its characters, making heroes and villains of those who went to fight. In other words, these two movies fought Vietnam all over again, taking different sides. Robert DeNiro, John Savage, and Best Supporting Actor Christopher Walken were the pals in *The Deer Hunter.* Jane Fonda, Jon Voight, and Bruce Dern were the political pawns in *Coming Home.*

Also Notable: *An Unmarried Woman, Superman, Heaven Can Wait, Interiors,* and *National Lampoon's Animal House.*

THE PLAYERS

Jane Fonda produced *Coming Home* and put a lot of her own brand of politics in it. She won her second Best Actress Oscar.

Jill Clayburgh was *An Unmarried Woman,* dumped by her wealthy New York husband, she had to find her own way. Clayburgh became a symbol to the Women's Movement due to this role.

Christopher Reeve picked up the role of *Superman* and flew with it.

MUSIC

Rock and roll superstar, considered "God" by many, Eric Clapton had a big hit with his "Lay Down, Sally."

Donna Summer's "Last Dance" was pure, unadulterated disco. Summer, herself, was the queen of the disco era.

Long Islander Billy Joel sang about midtown Manhattan and other crazy things on the *52nd Street* album.

Also Notable: John Travolta and Olivia Newton-John's hit from *Grease* was "You're the One That I Want"; Randy Newman's misunderstood "Short People" galled many listeners; country-gal Dolly Parton's big hit was "Here You Come Again"; Steve Martin's unusual "King Tut" was a novelty tune supreme.

LITERATURE

The World According to Garp was literature according to John Irving. This was a true crossover novel, both intellectuals and college students ate it up.

IN THE NEWS

Cult leader Jim Jones led hundreds of people to their deaths in one of the world's most talked-about mass suicides, the Jonestown massacre.

In California there was real estate tax revolt led by businessman Howard Jarvis, who wanted to pass Proposition 13.

The Camp David Accords were signed, making real heroes out of Jimmy Carter, Anwar Sadat, and Menachem Begin.

On April 26, the first anniversary party was thrown for Studio 54, the Sodom of midtown New York. If a bomb had dropped on famous West 54th Street that night, there would have been no one left to carry on. They were all there: Giorgio Armani, Halston, Perry Ellis, Calvin Klein, Reggie Jackson, Diana Vreeland, Francesco Scavullo, Peter Allen, and Yves St. Laurent. Studio 54 was the ground zero of American culture. Sex, drugs, and rock and roll were all in abundance. Everyone there was beautiful, and everyone who was beautiful was there. It would be the regular hangout for Liza Minnelli, Mick Jagger and his then wife Bianca, Truman Capote, and above all else Andy Warhol and his entourage.

SPORTS

Toothless Leon Spinks was all smiles as he won the heavyweight championship.

Notre Dame won the Cotton Bowl.

It looked like Joe DiMaggio's hitting record of 51 was going to be toppled by Cincinnati Red Pete Rose who connected in forty-four straight games. It all ended on August first when the streak was over.

TELEVISION

VCRs were appearing in more and more homes. A few short years earlier no one believed that they would be able to watch their favorite movie whenever they wanted. In the continuing feud between theatre owners and television programming directors, it must be noted that from this point on movie revival houses began to close. People were just as happy to see *Gone with the Wind* and *Casablanca* on the television screen instead of waiting for a revival house to show it.

"Three's Company" on ABC was a one-joke comedy that was a big hit. Two beautiful young women shared their apartment with a skirt-chasing guy who had to pretend he was gay. Lots of slapstick, otherwise it was flaccid entertainment.

"Mork and Mindy" on ABC starred Robin Williams as an alien from another planet. His verbal gymnastics, funny body language, and all-around brilliance made this show a refreshing departure from the usual sitcom. With Pam Dawber as Mindy, the two worked miracles together.

FADS AND FASHION

Toga parties hit college campuses.

1979

THE MOVIES

The China Syndrome directed by James Bridges. Nobody believed a thing like this could happen. It was all in the imagination of Hollywood: A nuclear power plant accident that led to near-disaster. Unbelievable! Just a few short weeks after this movie opened, the real thing occurred in a small town in Pennsylvania. At Three Mile Island, where the real disaster occurred, the death rate soared. At the box office, receipts did the same. Hollywood was leading viewers to think, finally, in the right direction. Jack Lemmon, Michael Douglas, and Jane Fonda helped raise these unsettling questions.

Alien directed by Ridley Scott. For the first time since the cheapies of the fifties, a female was the lead character in a science fiction film. Sigourney Weaver was the tall and silent type, a sort of female Gary Cooper. Of course, no one ever made Gary Cooper wear only his underwear in a scene. Women could be the leads of popular films, but men still made the movies and acted toward women in the old-fashioned way. The Women's Movement took one step ahead with this film . . . and one step back. This chiller was distinguished by Yaphet Kotto, John Hurt, Tom Skerrit, and some of the ugliest beasts ever on screen. In one famous scene, John Hurt proved to suffer from the worst case of indigestion ever screened.

Being There directed by Hal Ashby. Derived from the Jerzy Kosinski novel, this politically astute satire told the story of a men-

146

tally deficient man, Chance the gardener, who accidentally became the confidant of the president as Chauncey Gardner. All Chance wanted to do was watch television; he was like so many of his countrymen. Peter Sellers was brilliant as Chance. Melvyn Douglas turned in another great performance as a dying billionaire industrialist, and Shirley MacLaine shone as Douglas's wife.

Also notable: *All that Jazz, La Cage aux Folles,* Best Picture *Kramer vs. Kramer, Apocalypse Now,* and *Norma Rae.*

THE PLAYERS

Bo Derek was the latest beautiful blonde wife of actor John Derek. Bo followed in the high heels of Ursula Andress and Linda Evans. But she became her own woman, and many a man's fantasy, with *10.* Bo was all the things a perfect *10* represented.

Growing up as dummy Charlie McCarthy's human sister must not have been easy for Candice Bergen. Then, too, her early career as a model and sometime photographer didn't do much to make her a public figure outside of being Edgar Bergen's daughter. When she made *Starting Over,* she didn't have much to lose playing an off-key would-be singer. The movie made her a star in her own right.

Serious stage actress Meryl Streep always received good reviews. Now she was making films and getting Oscar nominations. After her Oscar-winning supporting performance in *Kramer vs. Kramer,* critics predicted even bigger things from her.

MUSIC

Disco hit its stride: The Village People, a group of singers dressed as Greenwich Village gay stereotypes, had a hit with their tongue-in-cheek "Y. M. C. A."

The California group The Eagles proved they had endurance with another chart-topping LP, *The Long Run.*

Michael Jackson's LP *Off the Wall* kept him on the charts.

Also notable: "I Will Survive" by Gloria Gaynor; Donna Summer's "Bad Girls"; the Doobie Brothers' "What a Fool Believes"; the arrival on the music scene of New York "punk" in the shape of Blondie.

LITERATURE

Writer Tom Wolfe wrote the not-altogether flattering portrait of America's one-time heroes, the original seven Mercury astronauts, in *The Right Stuff*. A large-scale reevaluation of what had been taken for granted was under way. Had the press conspired unwittingly with federal agencies to create media heroes? What was real? Who told the truth?

IN THE NEWS

On March 28, an accident at the Three Mile Island nuclear power plant in central Pennsylvania exposed thousands to radiation. It wasn't only in the movies anymore.

America was enduring a long spell of runaway inflation.

The federal government bailed out auto-maker giant Chrysler.

In November militant Iranian "students" seized the American embassy in Teheran (Terror-ran) and took some fifty embassy members hostage.

SPORTS

Yankee manager Billy Martin was fired after a fight had broken out between him and a marshmallow salesman in a Minnesota hotel.

Earvin "Magic" Johnson jumped to the attention of the public by scoring twenty-four points in the NCAA basketball final. His Michigan State team beat Indiana State 75–64.

TELEVISION

According to ABC News, all of America was "held hostage" by the Iranian students. This kind of panicky reporting was good for ratings and in fact led to "Nightline" with Ted Koppel being a late-night staple. Each night ABC drummed it into its audience the number of days the United States was being held captive. For instance, "America held hostage, day thirty-seven." Paranoia worked; America tuned in.

FADS AND FASHION

Writer Tom Wolfe called the Seventies "The Me Generation." As the decade closed, people were consumed by what was happening to them personally. The caring—or what passed for caring in the decade before—was now all self-directed. Transcendental Meditation or TM was practiced by many. So was EST. Actually everything spelled ME.

THE
1980s

Former Warner Brothers actor Ronald Reagan was elected president of the United States by soundly beating incumbent Jimmy Carter in November 1980. With his strongly conservative views, the new president ushered in a new era in American politics. His trickle-down theory of economics was matched by his up-by-the-boot-straps thinking.

The country, if not the world, was ready for a man like Reagan. His smooth demeanor and easygoing ways made him the "Great Communicator." The country had someone to look up to, and the nations of the world, by extension, looked to America for leadership.

America was ready to make money, and with Reagan in the White House it was able to wheel and deal. Reagan was president, but money was king. When the hit movie *Wall Street* opened, a line from the film could have been used to sum up the delirious decade of corporate mergers and acquisitions, "Greed is good."

An entire generation of Americans devoted to acquiring expensive cars, bigger homes, designer pets, and imported spring water emerged from obscurity: "Yuppies." They were young, upwardly mobile, urban professionals. They moved from their condo to their three-bedroom house to their mini-estate in a few short years. His hair was cut short; hers was cut bluntly. They collected *things*. While they may not have been desirable as friends, they embodied the cool, impersonal age. Their overt desire for all things of a certain status made them the envy of those who could not afford such luxury. College students aimed at being "Yuppies." A life built on credit debt seemed so attractive to those so young.

A mysterious new disease was being whispered about throughout the country. At first it was believed to be found only in certain groups, such as Haitians, hemophiliacs, and homosexuals. No matter who was struck, the new disease was fatal. Rumors piled on top of speculation on top of fear. When it was clear that the disease was communicable only through certain sexual activities, the religious Right was sure that these victims were being punished for their sins. In 1985 when popular television and movie star, as well as presidential friend, Rock Hudson was diagnosed with AIDS, the White House and the nation took notice. Soon Hudson was followed to his grave by scores of other celebrities, from Amanda Blake of "Gunsmoke" to flamboyant pianist Liberace to clothes designer Perry Ellis.

America was rethinking the sexual revolution. Active participation was drastically curtailed. A new outlet was opening up, however. The home video. People were able to stay at home and watch. And watch they did. Not only sex tapes, but the most recent movies, too. Hollywood had to change its thinking once again. The video explosion meant that fewer people were going into dark theatres, paying higher and higher prices to see what they could rent at home for a fraction of the cost of a movie ticket.

Rocking the entertainment industry, too, was the world of cable. The options for television viewing jumped from a relative few on the dial to an almost infinite variety of specials, twenty-four hour news broadcasts, sporting events, and music. MTV didn't seem like it could last. Who would want to watch music videos *all* day long? But the more sophisticated the videos became, the easier it was to accept MTV as a permanent presence on television. With stars such as Michael Jackson, Madonna, and Tina Turner, as well as such groups as Dire Straits and U2, music video had found a welcome home.

In sports, athlete's salaries continued to rise, while corporate sponsorship muscled into all forms of games and gaming.

The inflated prosperity of the decade came to a shocking end when the stock market crashed in October 1987. Real estate, which had soared throughout the decade, was one of the first to feel the economic downturn. The mini-estate that the "Yuppie" couple had purchased only a few years ago was now unable to be resold for its original price. Businesses trimmed back, reduced overhead and personnel. Belt-tightening was suddenly chic.

Vice President George Bush and his running mate Senator J.

Danforth Quayle were elected over their Democratic rivals in November 1988. In the political campaign of 1980 when Bush was running against Ronald Reagan for the Republican presidential nomination, Bush had dismissed Reagan's economic policies as "voodoo economics." Now George Bush inherited the residue of those very policies. More of a political appointee than a president, Bush and his side-kick Quayle ignored the pleading from the nation to do something about the ailing economy. Bush was "sick and tired" of hearing complaints about the hard economic times. Americans were baffled by their new president who obviously was nothing like their beloved former leader Ronald Reagan.

1980

THE MOVIES

Raging Bull directed by Martin Scorsese. Academy Award-winning Robert DeNiro played boxer Jake LaMotta in this brutally realistic and brilliantly realized film. Quoting from *On the Waterfront*, DeNiro as LaMotta played a scene as Brando contemplating how he "coulda been a contender." With fight scenes that were as glamorously photographed as they were grotesque with violence, the film was shot in black and white. Apparently that's how LaMotta saw the world.

Airplane! directed by Jim Abrahams, David Zucker, and his brother Jerry Zucker. A send-up of all the disaster movies, especially the too-earnest *Airport* series, this nonstop comedy was as nonsensical as it was funny. Commenting on all kinds of films, *Airplane!* spawned a series of films just like it. With Robert Hays, the priceless Julie Hagerty, and a supporting cast that resembled a reunion of old-time television actors, everyone lampooned themselves grandly. The TV veterans included Robert Stack, Lloyd Bridges, and Peter Graves.

The Rose directed by Mark Rydell. In a story that ripped off the life of Janis Joplin, Bette Midler gave her all as a drug-crazed, self-destructive and somehow loveable rock star. Midler was fierce and convincing in the film.

Also notable: *Coal Miner's Daughter, Fame, The Blue Lagoon, Melvin and Howard,* and *American Gigolo.*

THE PLAYERS

Goldie Hawn was pure gold in *Private Benjamin* and *Seems Like Old Times.* So bright and business shrewd, her own production company developed films for Goldie. She became one of the most bankable actresses in films.

Steve Martin played *The Jerk* very convincingly. His offbeat comic routines on television brought him to film stardom.

Also from television, now on film: Mary Tyler Moore was the despicable mother in Best Picture *Ordinary People,* a far cry from her wholesome, good girl image.

Also very hot: Richard Gere in *American Gigolo,* Robert DeNiro in *Raging Bull* and Brooke Shields in *The Blue Lagoon.*

MUSIC

Blondie was a featured performer on the soundtrack of *American Gigolo* and their hit "Call Me" rang up sales.

The boy from South Street in Freehold, New Jersey, Bruce Springsteen sang for his supper with "Hungry Heart."

The ballad "The Rose" was Bette Midler's big hit from the movie of the same name.

Also notable: "Fame," from the movie performed by Irene Cara; Diana Ross's "Upside Down"; "Whip It" by Devo (short for Devolution); John Lennon and Yoko Ono's *Double Fantasy* album; *The Wall* album by Pink Floyd; "Against the Wind" by Bob Seger and the Silver Bullet Band.

LITERATURE

The Official Preppy Handbook; the decade started off on the right tassled loafer. Here was a guide for those in the know and soon in the dough.

IN THE NEWS

President Carter promised to campaign for reelection from the Rose Garden until the hostages in Iran were freed. His term in office seemed to be trapped inside that faraway embassy.

In May, an attempt to rescue the hostages in Iran failed.

Massachusetts Senator Edward M. Kennedy decided to run against the incumbent for the presidency. Apparently he would only run for that office when it was against a fellow Democrat, having passed up the chance to take on a Republican four years before.

The Republicans put up former actor and former California Governor Ronald Reagan. His running mate was perennial political appointee George Bush, who was the former director of the CIA, and who had criticized Reagan during the primary campaign for his policy of "voodoo economics." The Republicans won over the stymied Democrats, wilting in the Rose Garden.

The volcano Mt. Saint Helens erupted in Washington state.

On December 8, outside his apartment at The Dakota in New York City, John Lennon was shot dead. With his death, the radical 1960s came to an ugly end.

SPORTS

Larry Holmes took Muhammad Ali to the cleaners and badly beat the former champ.

In Philadelphia there was an unusual joy: The Phillies won the World Series for the first time ever.

American speed skater Eric Heiden won five gold medals at the Lake Placid Olympics.

Bjorn Borg took on the fiery John McEnroe at Wimbledon and beat the American wise guy 1–6, 7–5, 6–3, 6–7 (16–18 in a tie-breaker), and 8–6.

TELEVISION

"Dallas" was not just another Texas city, it was a phenomenon on CBS on Friday nights. There had been prime-time soaps before, but this one had the whole country hooked. It was all about money and greed and power and occasionally real love. In other words, "Dallas" was just like America, or what America hoped it would be during the new decade. J. R. Ewing and his kin were the nastiest bunch of people on television outside Iran.

On November 21, the *Who Shot J. R.?* episode of "Dallas" garnered one of the biggest ratings in the history of television. Even people who weren't fans of the show needed to know who would be so bold as to shoot the nastiest man on television.

Media mogul Ted Turner of Atlanta had a little idea that could. It was Cable News Network or CNN, and it would telecast news twenty-four hours a day. "Too much," said the critics. Turner had the last laugh.

FADS AND FASHION

The Rubik's Cube had the country very nervous. People everywhere tried not to look stupid, but they did. The colorful plastic cube was nothing more than a brain-teaser for those with time and plastic on their hands.

1981

THE MOVIES

Reds directed by Warren Beatty. Never before had a mainstream American filmmaker taken the time and care Beatty did in bringing to the screen a sympathetic view of one man's Communism. John Reed, an early twentieth-century journalist, had written from inside the Kremlin about the Russian Revolution. This film was one part *Doctor Zhivago* and one part Social Studies 101, but one hundred percent enthralling. It featured Diane Keaton, Gene Hackman, Jerzy Kosinski, Jack Nicholson as Eugene O'Neill, and Maureen Stapleton.

Raiders of the Lost Ark directed by Steven Spielberg. A rehash of a 1940s serial, this movie firmly established the era of special effects and pyrotechnics. Loud and crass, it was just what the public wanted. Harrison Ford and hundreds of technicians filled in where writers once sat. The high cost of such movies were inevitably passed on to the ticket buyer.

Absence of Malice directed by Sydney Pollack. This was the flip side of *Raiders* . . . and it definitely belonged to a dying breed of films. A serious subject—journalistic responsibility—was crafted by experts and performed by professionals; it provoked thoughtful debates in its audience. But the performance at the box office is what mattered to Hollywood. This production and *Reds* were not smashes, whereas the frivolous Spielberg concoction was. The end result: more Spielberg; less intelligence at the movies.

Also Notable: *Ragtime,* which marked James Cagney's return to films; *Atlantic City, Arthur, On Golden Pond, S. O. B.,* and *Body Heat.*

THE PLAYERS

Susan Sarandon must have had it in her contract that she appear nude from the waist up. She did in the wonderful *Atlantic City* and people everywhere have had a new respect for lemons.

James Cagney was back from a twenty-year retirement and Milos Forman had him in *Ragtime.*

Warren Beatty directed himself and Maureen Stapleton of *Reds* to Oscar glory. He took home the statuette for Best Director. His date on Oscar night was Diane Keaton.

Katharine Hepburn won an unprescedented fourth Oscar for *On Golden Pond.*

MUSIC

All Olivia Newton-John wanted was to get "Physical." She capitalized on the trend of more and more Americans who joined gyms.

Teens to grandmothers somehow all enjoyed Blondie's big hit "The Tide is High." Who would have thought Debbie Harry would sail over to the mainstream?

George Harrison had a hit with his reminiscent "All Those Years Ago."

Kim Carnes made an old lady happy with her hit "Bette Davis Eyes." The old lady was Davis herself who always liked attention.

Also Notable: Stevie Nicks and Tom Petty dueted on "Stop

Draggin' My Heart Around"; Dolly Parton warbled "Nine to Five" from the film she made with Jane Fonda and Lily Tomlin.

IN THE NEWS

On January 20, as Ronald Wilson Reagan was being sworn into office as the fortieth United States president, a half a world away in Iran, the militant "students" were releasing the American hostages. Jimmy Carter—and by extension, America—had been finally humiliated worldwide.

On March 30, President Reagan was shot by a social outcast who wanted to impress actress Jodie Foster. Here was another frightening personality who wanted media attention to give his life meaning.

Secretary of State General Alexander Haig stated that he was "in control here" at the White House after hearing the news of Reagan's assassination attempt. A glance at the Constitution of the United States would have told him different. His attempt to reassure the nation was, in fact, a Constitutional fiasco.

Sandra Day O'Connor was appointed by President Reagan to the Supreme Court, thus becoming the first woman ever to be so honored.

SPORTS

Free agency compensation was the key issue in a fifty-day strike by baseball players, which ended on July 31.

In World Series play, the Dodgers beat the Yankees in a six-game tournament.

Trevor Berbick was the boxer who finally put an end to the career of Muhammad Ali.

Sugar Ray Leonard, who had won a gold medal in boxing at the 1976 Olympics, won the WBA junior middleweight title, and later in the year he won the welterweight championship.

Twenty year old Fernando Valenzuela was only a rookie pitcher, but he finished the season with an astounding 13–7 record.

TELEVISION

On January 12, "Dynasty" premiered. ABC's answer to the popular "Dallas," this Denver-based evening soap was just as greed-oriented as its CBS cousin, but it was far campier. Veteran actor John Forsythe joined aged-starlet Linda Evans and a host of youngsters who kept things rolling. It was not, however, until faded Elizabeth Taylor-wannabe Joan Collins hit the show as Alexis that the program really took off.

In March, Walter Cronkite the uncle figure to the nation, retired from his anchor spot on the "CBS Evening News." He was replaced by the less-than-avuncular, acerbic Dan Rather.

"Hill Street Blues" debuted on NBC on January 15. Gritty and realistic, the show was produced by Stephen Bocho, the new wunderkind of nighttime television. It was like no other cop show before. The cast included Daniel J. Travanti and Veronica Hamel.

"General Hospital" was the hottest daytime drama around, and its heat was generated by the Luke and Laura storyline.

FADS AND FASHION

Nancy Reagan's favorite color was red, thus "Nancy Reagan Red" became a favorite designer color. Women with lots of green in their purse could emulate the stylish First Lady.

Video games hit the arcades, and America's youth followed with coins in hand.

Nintendo was a video game played at home on the television. Pac-Man and Super Mario Brothers were other home entertainment favorites.

Designer jeans, such as those "designed" by Gloria Vanderbilt, were the "butt" of many jokes. Famous names appeared frequently on labels. Status symbols were now easily purchased at the mall.

Brooke Shields wouldn't allow anything to come between her and her Calvins. Her advertising campaign for the jeans was incredibly successful, even if it did take the credibility out of her acting career.

1982

THE MOVIES

Victor/Victoria directed by Blake Edwards. It was a gender-bender year at the movies. Transvestism was all in good fun: Julie Andrews played a woman playing a man playing a woman. The obvious jokes just kept rolling along, as did the musical numbers. Veteran Robert Preston was hysterical as a gay man in love with real-life former football star Alex Karras. The always-reliable James Garner and Lesley Ann Warren added to the fun.

Tootsie, directed by Sydney Pollack. Dustin Hoffman spent most of the film dressed as fictional soap star Dorothy Michaels. The film said more about men's feelings toward women than it did about men dressing as women, and the results were poignant and humorous. Teri Garr played Hoffman's doormat girlfriend while Jessica Lange played his idealized female. Bill Murray stole the show as Hoffman's snide roommate, Lange captured the Oscar for her supporting comedic flair.

An Officer and a Gentleman, directed by Taylor Hackford. Some actors were still dressing like men. Richard Gere starred in this straightforward love story between the title character and young factory worker Debra Winger. Many critics blasted this film for being sexist, as did costar Winger. They were probably right, but audiences ate it up.

First Blood directed by Ted Kotchoff. America was in the mood for a take-control action figure like Sylvester Stallone's Rambo. The Reagan-era hero was one who killed first and asked questions *never.* Stallone added Rambo to his skimpy list of hit performances, the other being Rocky Balboa. The actor would return to both characters time after time. Rambo spawned action-hero toys, which allowed the young to pretend they were blowing up hundreds of people.

Also notable: *Missing, The Verdict,* and the disturbing *Sophie's Choice.*

THE PLAYERS

Richard Pryor had been a stand-up comic who segued into films with a small role in *Lady Sings the Blues.* Now Pryor was hotter than a macadam road in August. His usual foulmouthed banter wasn't in evidence in the warmhearted *Busting Loose.*

Debra Winger was an angry young actress who impressed many in her first starring role in *Urban Cowboy* with John Travolta. She rose to stardom opposite Richard Gere in *An Officer and a Gentleman.* She resisted doing the scenes that were meant for the men in the audience. Her anger only made her performance better.

Paul Newman rose to the occasion in *The Verdict* in a role that nearly every older actor in Hollywood coveted. As the down-and-out attorney who needed to win a case, Newman was very effective. The one problem was that, even while drunk, he looked like Paul Newman.

MUSIC

Asia by the group of the same name was one of the best-selling LP's around North America.

White rhythm-and-blues duo Hall and Oates had a big hit with their "I Can't Go for That (No Can Do)."

The very moving movie *Chariots of Fire* spawned a hit instrumental, which was rousing and inspirational. Vangelis made a name for himself.

Also notable: Paul McCartney and Stevie Wonder blended their voices on "Ebony and Ivory," which had a good sentiment at its heart. It sounded, though, as if it had been sitting in someone's drawer for fifteen years.

LITERATURE

John Updike, chronicler of WASPish mores, turned fifty. *Bech is Back* was his birthday gift to the rest of us. His characters seemed haughty and aloof, not unlike their creator.

IN THE NEWS

On January 8, AT&T was busted up.

The Equal Rights Amendment for women was turned down by the states.

Gay-related immunodeficiency or GRID was a mysterious disease sweeping through the homosexual community.

Tylenol medications were tampered with causing a nationwide scare.

SPORTS

People were getting "nosey": it was reported that there was widespread use of cocaine in the NFL. So much for heroes. The game also endured a fifty-seven-day strike by players. What did those guys do during their layoff?

Ray "Boom Boom" Mancini beat Ernesto Espana for the middle-weight title.

Martina Navratilova was more than just a champion tennis player. She was now a certified media star, with articles prying into her personal life. What a life it was!

TELEVISION

"Family Ties" debuted on NBC on September 22. It commented on the decade in sitcom form. The parents (Meredith Baxter and Michael Gross) were aging members of the counterculture 1960s. Their children were materialistic sorts, in other words, children of the greedy 1980s. The parents were liberals, the eldest son was conservative. While the Keatons were fictional, audiences identified with the deep truth in their emotional lives. Michael J. Fox was the perfect "yuppie"-wannabe, and Justine Bateman epitomized the selfish, shallow, world-spinning-around-her adolescent. Tina Yothers played the youngest child, at least for a while.

"Cheers" debuted on the same network eight days later. Set in a bar in Boston, the show was an immediate hit with urban audiences, but it took time to gather steam across the country. Ted Danson was the reformed alcoholic Sam Malone, a former baseball player, and Shelley Long was a cultured, pseudointellectual, barmaid. The humor was honest, based on real characterization. The uniformly fine cast included Rhea Perlman as the disgruntled Carla; George Wendt as the perennially out-of-work Norm; George Ratzenberger as self-important Cliff; and Nicholas Colasanto as dim-witted Coach. Over the years the cast changed, but not the format, not the humor, not the basic barroom realism. Woody Harrelson and Kirstie Alley came later, but the brew remained heady.

"St. Elsewhere" premiered on NBC on October 26. The setting was a fictional Boston hospital. Unlike medical shows of the past, there was the new realism that the network had perfected in many of its shows. The topics weren't only tough, they challenged the viewer's thinking. Out went the traditional good-guy doctor. No one ever saw Dr. Kildare on these hospital floors. Denzel Washington and Mark Harmon did their residencies on this evening ward.

FADS AND FASHION

Giorgio Armani designed irresistible fashions for *American Gigolo,* and American men wanted to buy these.

Fitness was in. Men and women joined gyms, pumped iron, and got rock hard. They showed off their new forms with body suits, lycra pants, and big smiles.

Herpes was making the rounds.

Realism was making a comeback in the art world.

Shoppers were beginning to do more and more by mail. Why bother going to the mall when you can go to the mail?

Little blue Smurfs were everywhere. They even had an NBC show and their own language.

1983

THE MOVIES

The Big Chill directed by Lawrence Kasdan. Essentially a reunion film for the post-hip crowd who were approaching middle-age, the movie had a great soundtrack evocative of the 1960s. It was self-consciously cool and had an amazing cast of actors. Kevin Kline, Glenn Close, Jeff Goldblum, William Hurt, and Meg Tilly all shone. Kevin Costner played the suicide who brought them all together, but his footage was left on the cutting-room floor.

Terms of Endearment directed by James L. Brooks. Shirley Mac-Laine, Debra Winger, John Lithgow, Danny DeVito, and Jack Nicholson starred in this Best Picture three-hankie weeper that was given an edge by the devilish Nicholson. The two lead women seemed locked in mortal combat for scenes, keeping with their roles. MacLaine won the Oscar for Best Actress, and Nicholson was honored in the Best Supporting category.

Flashdance directed by Adrian Lyne. MTV had premiered two years before. It was definitely the precursor to this extended music video. It starred Jennifer Beals and Michael Nouri, both too perfect looking for anything but camera work. The musical numbers were fast and furious. The songs were what mattered; the plot was a silly string of clichés. But it was hot!

Also Notable: *The Right Stuff* from Tom Wolfe's book; the exposé

Silkwood; Woody Allen's answer to Warren Beatty's *Reds, Zelig;* and *King of Comedy.*

THE PLAYERS

He came from Down Under and went to the top: Mel Gibson had played *Mad Max,* and now he had American women madly in love with him in *The Year of Living Dangerously.*

Once part of the husband and wife team, Sonny and Cher, the female half decided she wanted to shed that variety show image. She wanted to act, *really* act. When she took the role of a lesbian in *Silkwood,* she convinced Hollywood she was serious. Still, the clothes she wore in public deprived her of the respect most talented thespians craved.

From "Saturday Night Live" to the movies. It was the scenario for many a young comic. But Eddie Murphy put his own stamp on it. In *Trading Places* he teamed with "SNL" vet Dan Aykroyd and claimed stardom.

LITERATURE

Stephen King had been scaring people half to death for quite a while. He checked in with *Christine* about a murderous car. Why not? Car insurance rates had been killing people for years.

MUSIC

The soundtrack for *Flashdance* was a giant crossover hit. Solidly based in the dreaded disco, it still appealed to black and white audiences and anyone who had an ear.

Lionel Ritchie's LP *Can't Slow Down* produced a slew of hits for the former Commodore lead singer.

Above everything else in music, though, was *Thriller* by Michael

Jackson. With this album Jackson zoomed to the top. His music videos were an integral part of the LP's success.

IN THE NEWS

On April 20, President Reagan bailed out Social Security. The president himself was seventy-two.

Sally Ride, the first woman in space, lifted off from Cape Canaveral, Florida, June 18.

The Big Three automakers reported an average 16.7 increase in sales for the year.

Computers were taking over the workplace.

AIDS replaced GRID. Autoimmune deficiency syndrome was an unwelcome addition to the American language.

On October 23, 241 Marines were killed in Beirut.

DRUGS

Angel Dust was the latest, greatest thing to hit the streets. Derived from animal tranquilizers, it became the urban drug of choice.

SPORTS

The new football league, the USFL, was launched with star Herschel Walker of the New Jersey Generals running the show.

The man just couldn't keep the job: Yankee manager Billy Martin was hired and fired within an eleven-month stretch.

Pine tar became a national issue. Using it was definitely not a smart idea. Just ask George Brett. Perhaps he should have been suspended, but he wasn't.

TELEVISION

On September 29, the last episode of "M*A*S*H" aired. It was the highest rated show in the history of television. All the loose strings were tied up, but America was at loose ends without the comedy.

The miniseries "The Winds of War" ran on ABC and drew huge numbers—and that was only the show's extras watching. In fact, the program renewed interest in the form that had fallen on mundane times. Robert Mitchum, sleepwalking through his role, was joined by Ali MacGraw, fast asleep in hers. Polly Bergen, John Houseman, and many, many, many others paraded across the tube.

"The Day After" was one of the most provocative TV movies ever aired. It was about the effects of nuclear war on America's heartland. Jason Robards, Jr., JoBeth Williams, and John Lithgow starred.

FADS AND FASHION

No self-respecting American parent would allow their child to be deprived of a Cabbage Patch doll. Any way that's how it seemed in 1983.

1984

THE MOVIES

Beverly Hills Cop directed by Martin Brest. Eddie Murphy took over the role that Sylvester Stallone gave up and ran with it. A simple story of a Detroit cop coming to the plush Southern California mecca was turned into something special with Murphy behind the wheel as Axel Foley.

Starman directed by John Carpenter. Basically, *E. T.* in human form, Jeff Bridges gave an endearing performance as the interstellar visitor. The feds were the heavies again—it's Hollywood shorthand for lack of better ideas—but this wasn't just another spaceship movie. Tender and sweet, it also benefited from the lovely Karen Allen as the very believable love interest. Carpenter who usually worked in horror films redeemed himself nicely.

Romancing the Stone directed by Robert Zemeckis. Kathleen Turner was a cautious romance novelist who found herself involved with Michael Douglas, a fortune hunter. Along the way they met the diabolical Danny DeVito. This was fast-paced entertainment in a fast-paced age.

Also Notable: *Places in the Heart, Country, The River,* (all country cousins to each other); *2010,* the weak follow-up to *2001; Ghostbusters, Splash,* and *The Terminator.*

THE PLAYERS

Those country girls: Sally Field, Jessica Lange, and Sissy Spacek. Each starred in their own down-home movie. In real life, farmers were losing the battle to remain independent; large corporations were buying up huge tracts of land and overly extended farmers were going bust. That lethal combination brought quite a lot of focus on their troubles. Hollywood, simultaneously trying to help out and cash in, came up with three different stories, all with a rustic theme. The three actresses were all Oscar-nominated. Sally Field won, and provided unintentional laughs when she gushed, "You like me. You *really* like me." Comics are still lampooning her "sincerity."

Daryl Hannah was the tall drink of water in *Splash*. She was unlike Hollywood blondes who came before her. She seemed ashamed to be so attractive and did things to draw attention away from her face.

Kathleen Turner had been steamy in *Body Heat,* but when she teamed up with Michael Douglas something happened to both of them. They were like old-time movie screen teams. They just clicked; they had chemistry. Whatever it was they suited each other.

MUSIC

When people heard "Like a Virgin," they thought it was a novelty song, a joke played on the radio. It was no joke. The one laughing the hardest was its singer, someone with the unlikely name Madonna. The "Material Girl" cranked out hit after hit. Like Michael Jackson, Madonna and the MTV generation were made for each other. Her controversial music videos were always on the cutting edge. These were downright entertaining even when their meanings were imperceptible. Madonna, herself, was very clear. She would do anything at any time to stay in the public eye. She single-handedly changed how "celebrity" status was thought of— she worked it.

Bruce Springsteen's *Born in the U. S. A.* LP came out at just the right time. That is, it was the right time for politicians to use the blue-collar ethics that the singer/songwriter espoused. Democrat and Republican alike wanted to be linked to Springsteen, who had tapped into the heartland of the country with this collection.

The *Private Dancer* album Tina Turner catapulted the singer into the stratosphere. Part rock legend, part sex symbol, and all-talented, Turner's brand of entertainment was this: Give them everything you got. She did, especially with the song "What's Love Got to Do with It?"

Also Notable: Prince was crowned the Little Richard of his day with his bizarre outfits and hit records, like "When Doves Cry"; England's Boy George was a cross-dresser, but his voice landed him on the charts with "Karma Chameleon." Rap music was making money for such artists as Run-D.M.C., the Fat Boys, and Kurtis Blow.

LITERATURE

America was reading Jackie Collins and Danielle Steel. These trashy novels, such as *Hollywood Wives* and *Star,* were pulp fiction at its most commercial.

IN THE NEWS

On April 26, President Reagan left for China. Who was more inscrutable?

On May 7, veterans of the Vietnam war reached an out-of-court settlement with drug companies relating to Agent Orange.

The Democrats nominated former Vice President Walter Mondale for the presidency. There was nothing surprising about that. His running mate caused the stir. For the first time in American politics, a woman was running for the vice presidency. Her name was Geraldine Ferraro.

In November the Democrats didn't have a chance. President Reagan was such a popular man that it would have taken Thomas Jefferson to unseat him. The former Hollywood actor parlayed his charm into victory.

SPORTS

The Los Angeles Olympics were the pride of the nation. However, not all countries would participate. The Soviets and many Eastern Bloc States passed up the event. That skewered things in our favor in terms of medal winning.

In football, Jim Brown's rushing record was shattered by Chicago Bear Walter Payton.

Mary Lou Retton won the gold medal in gymnastics at the L.A. Olympics. She was the first American woman to do it.

TELEVISION

They were America's dream family. Father was a doctor. Mother was an attorney. They lived in a beautiful brownstone. They wore great sweaters. Everybody wanted to be a member of the family. Amazingly, the family was black. "The Cosby Show" broke all the rules. When it premiered on September 20, it seemed like it would be just another family sitcom. It definitely was not. It was funny, warm, and hopeful. It was an inspiration.

"Miami Vice" had a great music score, terrific clothes, fast cars, and beautiful women. It also had Don Johnson and Phillip Michael Thomas. The combination was unbeatable.

FADS AND FASHION

People were asking, "Where's the beef?" It was an advertising slogan that passed into daily usage. The Democrats were asking the question of the Republican president.

"Baby Boomers" were coined as such. Who were they? Where did they come from?

The sexual revolution was slowing down due to AIDS.

A VCR arrived in nearly every home. Now America could watch Ingrid Bergman and Humphrey Bogart in *Casablanca* every night, right in the family room.

If "Baby Boomer" was a mystery to some, a "Yuppie" was easy to spot. Just look for the Ralph Lauren clothes, the BMW, and the job on Wall Street. Also the "Yuppie" (Young Upwardly Mobile Professional) lived in his/her/their dream condo.

"Miami Vice" had its own look. Sockless men, suits worn with T-shirts, pastel preferences. Oh, yes, razor stubble was found attractive.

1985

THE MOVIES

Prizzi's Honor directed by John Huston. The director was an old man whose career zenith had been years earlier. There was no reason to believe that he was still able to create this Mafia-lampoon, which was brilliantly on target. Jack Nicholson was a hit man for the mob, but then so was his love interest Kathleen Turner. Anjelica Huston (Oscar winner for her deft work) was the mob daughter, all gussied up and ready to do it on the rug. There was so much enthusiasm and fun in this film, it was almost sad when some of the characters got blown away.

Witness directed by Peter Weir. If it had been an American behind the camera, he could not have done better than this Australian. Weir captured the machinations of the Pennsylvania Dutch, the Amish. An updating of an old John Wayne Western, *The Angel and the Badman,* this was a typical fish-out-of-water story, but with loads of heart, mostly provided by Harrison Ford, Kelly McGillis, and Lukas Haas.

Jagged Edge directed by Richard Marquand. This movie began a lengthy series of "Did-he/she or didn't he/she do it?" Often on these projects, as on this one, the writer was a man named Joe Eszterhas, a guy with a gimmick. However, this was the first and it was nerve-wracking. Glenn Close and Jeff Bridges danced the deadly tango. (By the way, he did it.)

Also Notable: *Cocoon, Kiss of the Spider Woman, The Color Purple,* and the "Yuppie" Western *Silverado.*

THE PLAYERS

William Hurt could have had a nice career playing bland blonds. But he chose to be daring. His gay character in *Kiss of the Spider Woman* won him an Oscar and loads of fans.

Anjelica Huston had a few "strikes" against her: pluses which equalled minuses in Hollywood. She was the daughter of legendary director John Huston and the girlfriend of Jack Nicholson. Why should anyone take her acting seriously? After *Prizzi's Honor* they did. Huston had the right stuff and proved she was one of the finest actresses in the country.

Oprah Winfrey was a talk-show host from Chicago who played a small but significant part in *The Color Purple.* Audiences connected with her. Her humanity jumped right out and she became a star.

The Hollywood Brat Pack was a pale imitation of the old Rat Pack. Like that aged group, they made movies together. Emilio Estevez, Rob Lowe, Ally Sheedy, Judd Nelson, and Demi Moore terrorized the L.A. night scene.

MUSIC

Whitney Houston's first album *Whitney* synthesized the middle-of-the-road music of Dionne Warwick, her cousin, with pop/soul sounds.

"We Are the World" had nearly every recording artist imaginable harmonizing on it. Designed to earn money for African famine relief, it was a touching, moving recording.

The theme to "Miami Vice" was synthesizer fun.

Also Notable: A fund-raiser (for AIDS) "That's What Friends are For"; Wham's LP *Make it Big*. They didn't in America, although George Michael did as a solo act.

LITERATURE

Garrison Keillor, the hero of Lake Wobegon, was a radio fabulist. His tales were spun so cleverly no one knew he had made them up.

IN THE NEWS

On May 2, E. F. Hutton, one of the nation's largest brokerages, pleaded guilty to federal charges of manipulation. They paid $2 million in fines.

On July 13, "Live Aid" was broadcast on radio and television around the world. It raised $70 million for starving people in Africa. Phil Collins sang in England, hopped on an SST, and then sang in the U.S.A.

On October 2, television and screen legend Rock Hudson died of AIDS. His death from the disease reached into the hearts of many Americans who had always found the actor an affable personality. Hudson's close friendship with President Ronald Reagan brought the illness to the Chief Executive's door.

On December 11, the biggest corporate merger outside the oil industry occurred: General Electric agreed to purchase RCA for a reported $6.28 billion.

More farmers than ever were going broke.

President Reagan underwent surgery for cancer. His wife, Nancy, was getting attention, too. None of it was favorable. Her personality was coming under scrutiny and attack.

DRUGS

The UZI submachine gun emerges as drug dealers' weapon of choice.

SPORTS

William "Refrigerator" Perry was a 310-pound Chicago Bear tackle. He was transformed into a major endorsement machine.

The upstart United States Football League could not be saved. It fumbled and finally folded.

Kareem Abdul-Jabbar led his teammates, the L.A. Lakers, to their third NBA title in six years.

TELEVISION

"The Golden Girls" was really "Miami Nice." It recruited series veterans Bea Arthur, Rue McLanahan, Betty White, and Broadway's Estelle Getty. The jokes were racy, the situations believable, and the acting, especially by White, impeccable.

FADS AND FASHION

Kids were fast becoming part of the video generation. Music videos held the truths for the American young.

Andy Warhol discovered a street artist and made him famous: Jean Michel Basquiat.

1986

THE MOVIES

Platoon directed by Oliver Stone. The director's own drug-crazed life was the inspiration for this relentless examination of a grunt's life in Vietnam. Willem Dafoe, Tom Berrenger, and Charlie Sheen brought the horrors of war to the screen. The movie won the Best Movie Oscar and terrorized audiences.

Hannah and Her Sisters directed by Woody Allen. Allen's very neurotic New Yorkers were never so playful and enjoyable. Infidelity abounded. Allen was a classic showman. He had various characters involved with all sorts of artistic endeavors: acting, singing, painting, architecture, and even cooking. An enduring piece that's satisfyingly warm by its end. Michael Cain and Dianne Wiest won Oscars for their supporting roles.

Stand by Me directed by Rob Reiner. A group of young boys grow up in this remarkable, small, and touching movie. Someone's been murdered and the boys want to find the body. It's what young boys would really do. With Wil Wheaton, River Phoenix, and Corey Feldman. These boys were very recognizable.

Also Notable: *The Mission, Crocodile Dundee, The Color of Money,* and *Top Gun.*

THE PLAYERS

Out of the hordes of young men who were dominating movies, one stood out. He costarred with Paul Newman in *The Color of Money,* and jetted to stardom in *Top Gun.* Tom Cruise had the smile and the boyish looks to keep him flying. Incidentally, scuttlebutts claimed that Cruise's performance helped Newman finally win his long-elusive Oscar for Best Actor. Cruise's charm made older actors look good.

Sigourney Weaver battled one big mother in *Aliens* and came out alive. Her career was in very high gear.

Marlee Maitlin was the first hearing impaired actress to win an Oscar.

Dianne Wiest was the nutty New Yorker who found herself pregnant and happy at the end of *Hannah and Her Sisters.* For Wiest it was an impressive performance which lifted this stage actress to the foreground of films.

MUSIC

Paul Simon's *Graceland* became controversial even when it won award after award. It used many of South Africa's artists to promote the very American Simon.

Aerosmith and Run-D. M. C. recorded "Walk this Way," a trailblazing combination of styles and sounds.

Janet Jackson's *Control* showed off another Jackson to good advantage.

Also Notable: Anita Baker's "Rapture."

LITERATURE

Tom Wolfe's *Bonfire of the Vanities* had plenty of people talking. A big, sprawling story of corrupt New York, it spotlighted the very rich and the very poor. The novel hit people like lightning. Everybody read it.

IN THE NEWS

On January 20, Martin Luther King's birthday was observed as a national holiday for the first time.

On January 28, moments after lift-off the shuttle *Challenger* erupted into flames, killing the seven crewmen. The nation was shocked; the explosion had been televised live.

AIDS was not only killing Americans; it was destroying the health care system.

Tax reform was passed by the Senate.

It was not a good year on Wall Street. On November 14, Ivan Boesky agreed to plead guilty to insider trading. He had to pay $100 million in fines.

DRUGS

Cocaine use was widening, even with kids.

Boston Celtics star Len Bias died while freebasing.

"Crack" cocaine was becoming the ghetto drug of choice.

SPORTS

Mike Tyson knocked out Trevor Berbick in the second round to win the WBC title.

Middleweight boxer Sugar Ray Leonard came out of retirement to fight again, only to lose.

Forty-six-year-old golfer Jack Nicklaus had his best year in a long time. He won his twentieth major tournament in 1986.

TELEVISION

Across the country, on local channels as well as on public access cable, television evangelists were praying for God to save lost souls . . . and to fill their pockets with cash.

David Letterman was the king of very late-night television, since 1981. His NBC show followed the master, Johnny Carson, and featured "stupid pet tricks" and an assortment of crazy characters, like Larry "Bud" Melman. His humor wasn't for everybody, but then again not everybody stayed up that late.

On ABC Cybill Shepherd and Bruce Willis were starring in a concoction called "Moonlighting." Its infectious wit and style made it a real "Yuppie" comedy. Hung on the hook of a detective show, it was more than that. It was rarefied silliness with a twist of charm.

"L.A. Law" debuted on September 15. The stylish, post-"Perry Mason" view of lawyers and the law had a large and intriguing cast, including Harry Hamlin, Susan Dey, and Jimmy Smits. Not only were the cases involving, so were the personal lives of the attorneys. Nothing like this went on (as far as we know) between Perry and Della Street.

FADS AND FASHION

Americans were becoming more and more diet conscious, slimming down and staying that way. Nutrition was suddenly important.

Compact discs (CDs) replaced cassette tapes as the best way to listen to music.

1987

THE MOVIES

Fatal Attraction directed by Adrian Lyne. It was a story of the times. One sexual slip-up could mean doom. Instead of being about AIDS in a time of AIDS, this was about old-fashioned philandering. Michael Douglas had the perfect movie wife, Anne Archer, but strayed into the webbed fingers and arms of Glenn Close. And Close wouldn't take no for an answer when Douglas told her that he was still in love with Archer. This movie had audiences crouching on the floors of movie theatres in fear. It made millions at the box office and probably kept Close from attending quite a few parties. She was too convincing.

Broadcast News directed by James L. Brooks felt as if it were "The Mary Tyler Moore Show" grown older. Indeed Brooks worked on the old MTM production. Again set in a newsroom, the characters seemed familiar: the female news producer, the arrogant and empty newsman, and the gutsy but non-charismatic writer. Pulled off beautifully by its cast of Holly Hunter, William Hurt, and Albert Brooks, it was a comedy with plenty of bite. It also had Jack Nicholson in an unbilled cameo.

The Witches of Eastwick directed by George Miller. This movie had very little to do with John Updike's novel of the same name, but it had something Updike couldn't give it: sex appeal. Cher, Susan Sarandon, and Michelle Pfeiffer conjured up the devil, Jack Nicholson. The movie had too many vomit jokes, but loads of style and talent.

Also Notable: *Ironweed* with Meryl Streep and Jack Nicholson; *Moonstruck* with Cher, who walked away with the Best Actress Oscar; Woody Allen's *Radio Days;* and the last hurrah for John Huston, the brilliant *The Dead.*

THE PLAYERS

The coven of witches—Cher, Susan Sarandon, and Michelle Pfeiffer—gave moviegoers something to watch. Hot separately, together they were an inferno.

Glenn Close made her character Alex in *Fatal Attraction* multidimensional. She also broke loose from her uptight image to play sexy, and she was.

Robin Williams had been television's Mork. Now he was a star in movies, too, with *Good Morning, Vietnam.* After several lackluster films, Williams was allowed to play a character which let his brilliance shine. He was probably his generation's Charlie Chaplin.

MUSIC

Michael Jackson's *Bad* was real good news for sales. It debuted at number one on the charts.

U2 had a high-flying hit with "With or Without You."

New Jersey group Bon Jovi enjoyed success with "Livin' On A Prayer."

Also Notable: Terence Trent D'Arby was promoted and promoted as the next new superstar. It was all hype. "Gangstar" rap emerged in the form of Ice-T. With rumors of drug abuse all around him,

Bobby Brown exited the New Edition. Whitney Houston was still on the charts with "I Wanna Dance with Somebody." Brown and Houston eventually married.

LITERATURE

Toni Morrison published *Beloved,* and it became a best-seller. She was one of the first black authors to branch out into all markets.

IN THE NEWS

Perestroika was being mentioned on the lips of many who didn't know how to say it or what it meant. It was Soviet President Mikhail Gorbachev's plan at restructuring the Soviet Union.

Oliver North, who had come to fame for his role in the Irangate controversy, testified on national television. His boyish ways endeared him to a public unwilling to look past images and see the true nature of lies and, in this case, unconstitutional behavior.

President Reagan nominated Judge Robert Bork to the Supreme Court. Bork's extreme-rightist views made many people uncomfortable. A grass roots effort successfully blocked his place on the high court.

The nomination of yet another Supreme Court judge went up in smoke when it was discovered that Douglas Ginsberg smoked dope in college.

On Monday, October 19, the stock market fell an incredible five hundred points in one day. Called "Black Monday," it was the end of the spending, buying, and merging ways of the 1980s. From this day on, things wouldn't be the same for the American economy.

SPORTS

The New York Giants hadn't won a National League championship title since 1956. It was their year, though. They beat Denver 39–20. Quarterback Phil Simms completed twenty-two of twenty-five passes.

The America's Cup came back to the United States when Dennis Connor's *Stars & Stripes* beat its Australian competition, *Kookaburra III*.

Mike Tyson beat Tony Tucker in a twelve-round decision bout to win the IBF title. He thus became the first undisputed champ since Larry Holmes.

Magic Johnson and his Lakers beat the Boston Celtics, led by Larry Bird, for the NBA title.

TELEVISION

The Fox network had to be different. To compete with the "Big Three" was crazy in the first place, but to play at the very same game was suicidal. The executives at the fourth network planned a revolutionary idea: relate to the public's lowest common denominator. Sex sells. In that spirit "Married . . . with Children" was born.

After several seasons on the tube, "Wheel of Fortune" brought back the enthusiasm for the game show. With Pat Sajak and Vanna White spinning her letters, America tuned in night after night.

Jim and Tammy Bakker went off the air in scandal, both financial and personal. The two evangelists elicited public sympathy, especially with Tammy's manufactured tears. Still Jim went to jail.

FADS AND FASHION

The "New Age" was here. Faith healers, channelers, space travelers, and crystals were all part of this trend. Ask Shirley MacLaine who wrote several books, one of which was an ABC miniseries.

People who watched television now had a new name. They were now dubbed "Couch Potatoes."

Christian Lacroix had bad timing. He introduced a line of pouffy skirts with petticoats and bustiers. He believed the party times were never going to change, things would only get more outlandish. They didn't bounce right back after the stock market crash. Even New York financier Donald Trump could have told the designer that.

1988

THE MOVIES

Working Girl directed by Mike Nichols. Savvy chick from Staten Island found herself at the mercy of her devious big city woman boss. Romance was in the form of Harrison Ford. It was fun and diverting, although it may not have had all the corporate politics right. After all, it had a sitcom ending. Melanie Griffith and Sigourney Weaver worked great together, though. Carly Simon supplied the score.

Dangerous Liaisons directed by Stephen Frears. It was sexy and hot . . . and everyone kept their clothes on. Sure there was plenty of heavy breathing and billowing bosoms, but this was France in the 1700's. Glenn Close schemed with John Malkovich, and Michelle Pfeiffer suffered at their dirty hands. The most remarkable thing, this movie was made on a relative shoe-string budget, and no one could tell.

Rain Man directed by Barry Levinson. Dustin Hoffman was matched with Tom Cruise. Their noses made it seem as if they could be brothers, as indeed that's what they played. Hoffman was a savant, much like Peter Sellers in *Being There*. Cruise was his smart, savvy savior who never knew his older brother existed. It was a road movie, a buddy movie, and 1988's Best Picture. Cruise once again proved to be a lucky charm. His empathy helped Hoffman shag the Oscar for Best Actor.

Also Notable: *Mississippi Burning,* which reconstructed the new South's recent history; Oscar-winning Jodie Foster in *The Accused; A Fish Called Wanda; Big; Who Framed Roger Rabbit?;* and *Bull Durham.*

THE PLAYERS

Hot after the previous year's double-bill hits, *No Way Out* and *The Untouchables,* Kevin Costner solidified his newfound stardom with *Bull Durham.* Baseball movies were deemed fatal. Costner knew better.

Melanie Griffith was the daughter of Tippi Hedren, star of *The Birds.* Griffith had acted since she was a teenager, but with *Working Girl* she became her own working woman.

Kevin Kline had won a Tony Award on Broadway and appeared in many movies, never to great acclaim. But when the multi-talented Kline played Otto in *A Fish Called Wanda,* he had the room he needed to be funny and maniacal. He won a well-deserved Oscar for his supporting role in *Wanda.*

MUSIC

George Harrison's "Got My Mind Set on You" rocketed the former Beatle back up the chart.

INXS hit number one with their "Need You Tonight."

Whitney Houston continued her long string of number ones with "So Emotional."

Also Notable: Now out on his own and looking for a "Father Figure," George Michael had a big winner. Redheaded Rick Astley had several big songs, including "Together Forever." Lip-synching Milli Vanilli's "Girl You Know It's True" turned out to be all false.

LITERATURE

Tom Clancy's brand of hard-driven fiction appealed more to men than women, who were the traditional book-buyers. That didn't prevent him from being a best-selling author, however. His *Hunt for Red October* caused quite a few eyebrows to be raised: How did he know only what the Navy knew?

IN THE NEWS

Abortion was becoming the new civil war. Pro-life and pro-choice factions fought this very personal issue very publicly.

The Democrats nominated Massachusetts Governor Michael Dukakis for the presidency. His running mate was Texas Senator Lloyd Bentsen.

Vice President George Bush easily won his party's nomination with the hope of continuing the legacy of the Reagan reign. His surprising running mate was a little known Indiana Senator J. Danforth Quayle. Political insiders considered Bush's choice a way of making him "assassination proof."

A highlight of the campaign was the vice presidential debate wherein Bentsen said to Quayle, "I knew Jack Kennedy. He was a friend of mine. And believe me, you're no Jack Kennedy."

DRUGS

Artist Jean Michel Basquiat died of a heroin overdose. The former street artist had made a distinguished reputation for himself as well as lots of money.

SPORTS

In August, heavyweight champ Mike Tyson broke his hand on the face of a man outside a nightclub; while in the ring, Tyson did better by putting Michael Spinks out of commission within ninety-one seconds.

At the Olympics, U. S. skater Brian Boitano outskated Brian Orser of Canada to win the gold medal.

Wayne Gretzky left his Edmonton hockey team to join up with Los Angeles.

Florence Griffith-Joyner took home three gold medals and one silver at the Seoul Summer Olympics.

TELEVISION

Trash TV was finally here. The jokes that Paddy Chayefsky made in *Network* were all coming true. With the likes of "Geraldo," and "Hard Copy," America was getting blood and guts and drivel on a nightly basis. The ratings for these shows soared. Give the public what they want, programmers thought, and you won't go broke.

On ABC "Roseanne" continued to be as big a draw as its star Roseanne Barr. Unlike the blue-collar Bunkers of "All in the Family," the Conners were definitely and openly a matriarchal group.

FADS AND FASHION

The success of *Who Framed Roger Rabbit?* flooded the market with spin-off merchandise.

1989

THE MOVIES

Field of Dreams directed by Phil Alden Robinson was every boy's dream come true. It was, in fact, a tearjerker for men. Kevin Costner starred in his second successful baseball movie in as many years. The guy knew how to pick winners, but this certainly didn't have the traditional sign of a hit. A man hears a voice that tells him to build a baseball field. "Build it and they will come." They do. Audiences went to *Field of Dreams* in teams.

Born on the Fourth of July directed by Oliver Stone. Based on the book by Vietnam veteran, wheelchair-bound Ron Kovic, Stone wanted America to forever atone for its past sins. He was relentless in his pursuit of accountability. He did draw a fine performance out of pretty boy Tom Cruise, who was amassing a sizable string of solid hits.

Do the Right Thing directed by Spike Lee. Fear shot through Hollywood executives. The plot centered around an incipient race riot, and many believed that the movie would trigger just what it displayed on screen. Director Lee handled the tough subject very sensibly. Danny Aiello, Ossie Davis, and the brilliant Samuel L. Jackson participated in this confrontation.

Also Notable: the Civil War battle film *Glory,* Woody Allen's *Crimes and Misdemeanors, Sex, Lies and Videotape,* and *The Fabulous*

Baker Boys. The War of the Roses may have been the decade's headstone. *Batman* set all-time box office records.

THE PLAYERS

When Michelle Pfeiffer sang "Makin' Whoopee" in *The Fabulous Baker Boys,* she reminded movie fans of Rita Hayworth singing "Put the Blame on Mame." In other words, she defined female sexuality for her time.

It was a supporting role in a big movie. The character died. Roles like this one had made stars of actresses before. But Julia Roberts probably would have become one without *Steel Magnolias.* Her smile and her charm couldn't have gone unnoticed for long.

Denzel Washington was a New York stage-trained actor with the Negro Ensemble Company. He had appeared in several films before and had been nominated for *Cry Freedom,* but when he was bull-whipped in *Glory,* he jumped off the screen. He was honored with a statuette for Best Supporting Actor on Academy Award night.

MUSIC

"The Living Years" by Mike and the Mechanics was probably responsible for more family reunions than any other rock song. The idea was: Don't let time go by without telling someone you loved them.

Bette Midler checked in with a hit after a long absence from the charts. Her "Wind Beneath My Wings" had the Divine Miss M vocally soaring.

Prince had a novelty hit from the movie *Batman.* His "Batdance" was a strange number that had to be seen on video for its full effect.

Also Notable: Billy Joel's "We Didn't Start the Fire," about, well, the things that happened since 1950; "Hangin' Tough," by the New Kids on the Block; Madonna's "Like a Prayer."

LITERATURE

Salman Rushdie's *The Satanic Verses* sure got that guy in trouble! Ayotollah Khomeini put a contract out on the guy for besmirching the Muslims.

IN THE NEWS

The *Exxon Valdez* ran aground in Alaska spilling millions of gallons of oil. Plant and wildlife were affected for years to come.

On June 4, the massacre in Tiananmen Square was broadcast live.

Newly inaugurated President Bush promised a "kinder and gentler nation."

William Bennett was appointed "drug czar." Bennett had once dated Janis Joplin.

In November, the Cold War came to a close after a long-running forty-four years. The Berlin Wall was dismantled. Capitalism was spread by selling chunks of the wall.

SPORTS

Los Angeles Raider's, Art Shell became the first black head coach of the postwar era.

At the Super Bowl, the San Francisco 49ers eked past Cincinnati to score a 20–16 victory.

The earthquake in San Francisco killed sixty-one people and postponed the World Series for over a week. It was a hometown game, however, and Oakland defeated the Giants.

TELEVISION

Arsenio Hall brought a black urban hipness to late-night television with his talk show.

Fox television premiered "In Living Color," a racially edgy comedy show with a big attitude. It was tasteless; it was funny.

FADS AND FASHIONS

The *Batman* craze took wing.

THE
1990s

Cutbacks, down-sizing, and lay-offs were part of the American way of life as the country staggered into the new decade. Caught in a recession that would not go away, America needed to break with its recent past. The lucky recipient of this mood swing was Governor Bill Clinton of Arkansas, who easily beat incumbent George Bush in a three-way race for the White House. The third man in the race was independent H. Ross Perot who was as icono clastic as he was homespun. That odd combination was enticing, but not so appealing that the American voting population would hand over the highest job in the land to a relative unknown from Texas.

Ironically, some people were not only getting rich, they were getting far richer. Entertainment conglomerates were signing large deals with the likes of Madonna, Michael Jackson, and Barbra Streisand, ensuring that these celebrities would not only remain in the public eye, but also control their own professional destinies. The importance of staying on top was never more important; there were so many more on the bottom.

Sequels continued to dominate Hollywood. In an era where everything needed to be safe, from sex to investments, the safest bet for Hollywood was the tried and true. Capitalizing on solid hits was nothing new to the film industry, but now it appeared to be their only impulse.

A small-budgeted, independent film from Great Britain, *The Crying Game* caught the attention of filmgoers, earning its producers millions of American dollars. It was completely different from the homogenized blockbusters that Hollywood kept cranking out. Its clever marketing and controversial plot twist paid off for its foreign backers.

Talk shows were never more popular. Oprah Winfrey, Phil Donahue, Geraldo Rivera, and Jay Leno were the brightest stars of the genre, but they certainly were not alone. There were talk shows all over the dial. Every nuance of American life could be scrutinized for sixty minutes on these programs. Only Leno and Arsenio Hall offered traditional entertainment shows. It was not unlikely to hear about lesbian adoptive parents, a shapely nude model who had once been a man, or any other facet or proclivity of human sexuality. After all, it was the 1990s, people were playing it safe sexually. They still wanted to hear about it even if they were not doing it.

The AIDS epidemic had become so ingrained in the American psyche that the Pulitzer Prize for drama was given in 1993 to Tony Kushner for his epic play, *Angels in America*. The new openness of sexual expression for gays and lesbians was never more apparent than their march on Washington. Still the ban on gays and lesbians in the military dominated domestic policy making.

Rodney King's video taped beating by Los Angeles police officers played on news broadcasts around the world. When his attackers were acquitted, riots broke out in the City of Angels, sparking a too long-ignored debate about race relations in the country.

Women's rights advocates numbered among the supporters of the president and his outspoken wife, Hillary Rodham Clinton. But the chief executive had difficulty finding appropriate female candidates to fill certain federal positions. Women were still being treated by a different code of ethics than the male counterparts in equal job slots.

There was nothing that kept men and women from being "Couch Potatoes," those lovable do-nothings who sat and watched television hour after hour. The sedentary life was attractive to those who did not or would not participate in sports. With the coming of "digital interactive multimedia," nothing was too far from the remote control. The new technologies are both high- and low-tech. Among the low-tech, people can use remote-control pads to play along with the popular television quiz show "Jeopardy!" Other advanced technologies go beyond escapism, allowing cable subscribers with personal computers to browse through libraries, hold conferences, and play games with partners across the continent.

1990

THE MOVIES

Dances with Wolves directed by Kevin Costner. The talk about the movie wasn't good. It was called, behind the director's back, *Kevin's Gate,* a reference to the disastrous *Heaven's Gate* of 1981. When had a Western, a *real* Western, been successful? Not for many years. The youth audience didn't even know what one was. It would take careful marketing to make this baby dance. Whatever the maneuverings, the film was a huge hit and a major critical success for the first-time director. His instincts were among the best in the business and he proved it once again. Costner starred with Mary McDonnell. He won the Oscar for Best Director and his movie was honored as Best Picture.

Goodfellas directed by Martin Scorsese. Small-time hoods have always made for a good story. With Ray Liotta, Robert DeNiro, and Oscar-winning Joe Pesci, this movie was ugly, unnerving, and very realistic. Pesci, in particular, was despicably good.

The Grifters directed by Stephen Frears. Based on the book by Jim Thompson, here were more small-time crooks, but director Frears gave this film a "noir-ish" edge. In many ways it was the daughter of *Double Indemnity,* with Anjelica Huston aping Barbara Stanwyck's toughness right down to the dyed blond hairdo. Annette Bening and John Cusack took part in the celluloid con. You may never look at a bunch of oranges the same way again.

The Adventures of Ford Fairlane directed by Renny Harlin, starred Andrew Dice Clay, the crude and rude stand-up comic. The movie, like the star, was sophomoric and amateurish. What makes this movie memorable is how Hollywood would bank on an improbable star and lose big-time. The movie, again like its star, is more of an embarrassment to business ethics than to good taste.

Teenage Mutant Ninja Turtles directed by Steve Barron. Crimefighting giant turtles live in the sewers of New York and talk as if they were surfer dudes from L. A. It made sense to little children who bought the toys that were part of the Ninja Turtle tie-in.

Also Notable: Warren Beatty and Madonna were in *Dick Tracy,* he directed, she tried to act. Julia Roberts cavorted in *Pretty Woman.* Ghosts resurrected "Unchained Melody."

THE PLAYERS

Richard Gere's career came back from the dead when he costarred with Julia Roberts in *Pretty Woman.* Her beaming smile made his dour expressions seem perplexed. Maybe he was trying to analyze how she was becoming the biggest star of the decade.

Joe Pesci appeared in both *Goodfellas* and the vastly popular *Home Alone.* His versatility put him over the top. His young costar in *Home Alone,* however, needed to do only one thing: be cute. And that's what made Macaulay Culkin a star.

MUSIC

One queen stole from many: Madonna purloined the dance club craze for her song "Vogue" from black drag artists. Her references to nearly every hot movie icon made this big campy news.

Whitney Houston kept belting out hit after hit. "I'm Your Baby Tonight" was her big one for the year.

Mariah Carey had a spectacular voice that rose over such material as "Vision of Love."

Also Notable: Country music was inching its way into the mainstream. Wilson Phillips (children of the Mamas and the Papas and the Beach Boys) had a hit with "Hold On." Another second-generation star group was Nelson, the twin sons of Rick, who had a hit with "Love and Affection."

LITERATURE

The cult of Anne Rice caught fire with *The Witching Hour.* Rice's stories of depravity, yearning, and the supernatural made her one of the nation's favorite writers. Spooks and sex mixed for success.

IN THE NEWS

Washington, D.C., Mayor Marion Barry was caught smoking crack in an FBI sting operation. The whole thing played on television.

The recession deepened as the Republican administration ignored it.

Vice President Dan Quayle continued to come under attack for his naive answers to hard questions.

One in four black men in their twenties was either behind bars, on probation, or on parole.

SPORTS

College basketball heated up interest across the nation, but it was the University of Nevada at Las Vegas over Duke in the exciting final.

For the ninth time, Martina Navratilova won the U.S. Open. Pete Sampras was the men's winner.

The Cincinnati Reds bested the Oakland A's in a big upset World Series. The Reds swept 4–0. Even MVP Ricky Henderson couldn't help his Oakland teammates.

The San Francisco 49er's won the Super Bowl for the fourth time, tying the Pittsburgh Steelers' record. The Denver Broncos were trampled by the California team.

TELEVISION

"Northern Exposure" debuted on CBS and quickly became a "Yuppie" hit. Another fish-out-of-water scenario, a New York doctor was assigned to a small town in Alaska to pay for his schooling. The cast members were all adept at playing eccentrics. Rob Morrow, Janine Turner, and John Corbett led the pack.

"Beverly Hills, 90210" was a Fox network hit that introduced an entire new breed of young stars to television. Jason Priestley, Shannen Doherty, and Luke Perry were slightly long in the tooth to play teenagers convincingly, but they were good-looking enough to draw tons of fans. It was pure escapism to watch rich Beverly Hills kids go about their lives.

"The Simpsons" were physically cartoons, unlike their human counterparts on so many sitcoms. But their behavior was more human than most. Their idiosyncracies struck a chord. Their brat son Bart was very much like real young boys, not the kinds usually seen on bland TV. Dad was Homer and Mom was Marge; any resemblance to "Ozzie and Harriet" was purely coincidental.

"Twin Peaks" debuted on April 9 and caused a sensation. The plot was unusual, the camera-work was unusual, the acting was *very* unusual. Filmmaker David Lynch's disturbed view of suburban life seemed to be a winner. But the show quickly ran out of steam even though it had a stellar cast, including Kyle MacLachlan, Peggy Lipton, and Michael Ontkean. At first a limited series, the audience lost interest once it became a weekly show.

TEEN IDOLS

Luke Perry, Jason Priestley, and Shannen Doherty acted out the ultimate wish fulfillments for 1990's American youth on "Beverly Hills, 90210": They were rich and good-looking, and their futures seemed especially bright.

FADS AND FASHION

Black fashions were crossing over: whites wore twisted braids, dreadlocks, and hi-tops.

Bart Simpson appeared not only on TV but on lunchboxes, bedsheets, and in the dreams of children across the country.

1991

THE MOVIES

The Silence of the Lambs directed by Jonathan Deeme. This flick crossed a lot of boundaries. It was a mainstream Hollywood production that incorporated elements of horror movies so effectively that all kinds of people congregated in the audience. It was a true crossover hit. Serious moviegoers—as well as those looking for the cheap thrill—found what they were looking for. A young FBI agent was tracking a serial killer. To understand what goes on in a madman's mind, she meets a real madman, Hannibal the Cannibal Lecter. Jodie Foster and Anthony Hopkins were so good, they both won Oscars, as did the movie, its screenplay, and direction.

JFK directed by Oliver Stone. The country had gone wild with conspiracy theories about the assassination of the thirty-fifth president. Kevin Costner played discredited New Orleans District Attorney Jim Garrison. Plenty of liberal-thinking do-gooders participated in cameos. Jack Lemon, Walter Matthau, and Donald Sutherland were among them.

Bugsy directed by Barry Levinson. The life and times of racketeer "Bugsy" Siegel were elegantly brought to the screen by director Levinson and producer/star Beatty. Harvey Keitel, Ben Kingsley, and Annette Bening re-created the gangster era.

Also Notable: young filmmaker John Singleton's *Boyz N the Hood; Terminator II: Judgment Day* with Arnold Schwarzenegger, which was probably the last word in action films; *New Jack City,* a film that incited quite a lot of violence in the theatre, not only on the screen; Spike Lee's *Jungle Fever;* and the girl-buddy movie *Thelma and Louise,* a feminist take on *Butch Cassidy and the Sundance Kid.*

THE PLAYERS

She had class and good looks. She had talent, too. Above all else she had a romance with Warren Beatty. But then, what attractive actress hadn't? But she was different. She landed him. She was Annette Bening, and now she was Mrs. Warren Beatty, mother of his daughter.

Jodie Foster started out acting as a very young child. She played a teen hooker in *Taxi Driver,* won an Oscar for *The Accused,* but firmed up superstar status when she played Clarice Starling in *The Silence of the Lambs.* It didn't hurt that she also directed the well-respected *Little Man Tate.*

Anthony Hopkins was the thinking-woman's sex object. He had kicked around movies for years, but never had his defining moment. It finally came. His Hannibal Lecter was as memorable as any character put on screen.

MUSIC

Madonna's sultry "Justify My Love" was a better video than a song, but it still was a hit.

"More Than Words" by Extreme gave the Boston-based band a solid hit. The group's sound was very reminiscent of the Everly Brothers.

Natalie Cole's remake of her father's hit "Unforgettable" gave her the recognition that had eluded her for years.

Also Notable: Michael Jackson's "Black or White," Prince's "Diamonds and Pearls," and EMF's "Unbelievable."

LITERATURE

Scarlett by Alexandra Ripley continued the story begun by Margaret Mitchell in *Gone with the Wind.* No matter how hyped it was, no matter how many copies it sold (plenty), Ripley was no Mitchell, and this was not a satisfying sequel to one of the most beloved books in American history.

John Grisham's *The Firm* launched one of the most phenomenal careers in American writing. In a few short years, this Southern attorney became a multimillionaire with both book and movie deals.

IN THE NEWS

On January 17, America launched its attack on the totalitarian regime of Iraq, a country that had invaded its neighbor Kuwait. President Bush said that the "aggression could not stand." American troops were led by the charismatic General Norman H. Schwarzkopf who became a national hero. Chairman of the Joint Chiefs of Staff, General Colin Powell, a black man, also succeeded, not only capturing targets, but in gaining the attention of the public. Operation Desert Storm was underway.

The president's approval rating was at an all-time high.

Neo-conservative Clarence Thomas was nominated to be a Justice on the Supreme Court bench. Thomas's rise from poor boy to a position of power was looked upon by many as the route blacks ought to take to gain a power base. In hearings broadcast to the nation, however, Thomas had to defend himself from Anita Hill who accused her former boss of sexual harassment.

SPORTS

Michael Jordan led the Chicago Bulls to the NBA title over the L.A. Lakers.

Basketball superstar Magic Johnson announced that he was HIV-positive. His words awakened thousands of heterosexuals to the dangers of AIDS.

Mike Powell broke Bob Beamon's "unsurpassable" long-jump record. On August 30 he went the distance and set a new world's record at 29 ft. 4 1/4 in.

TELEVISION

"Family Matters," one of ABC's Friday night family-oriented shows, featured Steve Urkel, the first black nerd on television. Progress?

"Murphy Brown" starring Candice Bergen was a hit Monday night show on CBS. It was followed by "Designing Women," a comedy about four southern belles. One of them, Delta Burke, feuded openly with the producers of the show. More ink was spilled about that skirmish than about the Civil War.

FADS AND FASHION

Torn jeans were in. Not jeans that had been worn and torn. No, new jeans were purchased already torn.

Grunge was not only acceptable, it was a proud statement. Perhaps taking a cue from so many homeless people on the streets, young people began to dress down. *Way down.* Seattle was the spawning ground of much of this fashion. Nirvana and Pearl Jam were grunge heroes.

1992

THE MOVIES

Basic Instinct directed by Paul Verhoeven. Seldom had a movie received so much pre-release publicity. And all of it was bad. This flick pushed the envelope of what was acceptable. Audiences flocked to the theatres, proving once again that American tastes run as low as mud in the Mississippi. Michael Douglas was back in his typical bland and blank role. He was paired with Sharon Stone, one of the hottest actresses to appear on celluloid. Stone left nothing to the imagination. She apparently wanted the job so bad she said yes to anything. *Anything.* The plot was convoluted and could have been a real thriller, but everyone including top-dollar screenwriter Joe Eszterhas ran out of ideas. The ending, like most of Douglas's scenes, was flaccid.

Unforgiven directed by Clint Eastwood. You could argue Hollywood only liked aging cowboys. Eastwood's professional point came late in the season, as did John Wayne's. The film garnered award after award for playing down Eastwood's famous fervor for violence. Yes, it was bloody, but bloody with a point. Gene Hackman renewed his credentials as a top-drawer actor and won the Best Supporting Actor nod. Morgan Freeman and Richard Harris appeared in roles that could have been played by anyone in the Screen Actors Guild. Eastwood clutched two Oscars for his efforts: Best Director and Best Picture.

Husbands and Wives directed by Woody Allen. The publicity surrounding this movie was unadulterated sensation. The movie
turned out to be quite mediocre. Woody Allen and Mia Farrow
costarred, probably for the last time. They portrayed New Yorkers
who were once in love and were now out of love. If nothing else, it
was timely.

Also Notable: Seldom had an art-house film captured the imagination of the vast movie audience, but *The Crying Game* did just that.
The Last of the Mohicans, Al Pacino's Oscar-winning *Scent of a
Woman*, and Jack Nicholson in *A Few Good Men*, with Tom Cruise
and Demi Moore.

THE PLAYERS

Mia Farrow found herself in yet another scandal involving a much
older man and a young woman. This time, though, she was the injured party. Her adopted daughter Soon-Yi was involved in an affair with Farrow's longtime companion, filmmaker Woody Allen.
The story of would-be child abuse and infidelity would have been a
good plot if it weren't so very sad for the children involved.

Demi Moore and Bruce Willis were *the* Hollywood couple, but
Moore's nude appearances on the covers of magazines gave more
than enough exposure to a couple of other things.

Daniel Day Lewis went from thinking man's movies to screen
hunk with *The Last of the Mohicans*. He was now a big box-office
draw as well as a brilliant theatrical presence.

MUSIC

Whitney Houston acted in and sang on the soundtrack of *The
Bodyguard*. From that recording came her mega-hit, written by
Dolly Parton, "I Will Always Love You."

Eric Clapton was *Unplugged* and had another hit with his "Layla."

British singer Annie Lennox's soaring voice made everything she recorded listenable, but her "Walking on Broken Glass" was bloody good.

Also Notable: Garth Brooks's LP *The Chase;* Billy Ray Cyrus's *Some Gave All;* and fake-soul singer Michael Bolton continued to amaze critics with his hits, including those from his *Timeless* album.

LITERATURE

Robert James Waller's *The Bridges of Madison County* was a sensation. The small love story about a photographer and a lonely Iowa housewife struck a chord deep within the hearts of book-buying Americans.

IN THE NEWS

President Bush reacted to questions about the deepening recession by saying he was "sick and tired of carping little Democrats complaining about the economy." Things were getting worse.

A fictional character was big news in 1992. Television's "Murphy Brown" was having a child without benefit of marriage. Vice President J. Danforth Quayle condemned the bastard child as well as those he claimed were part of the "cultural elite," who allowed such things to happen. Murphy Brown and her problems were the work of writers; actual single mothers had no one writing their lines.

Vice President J. Danforth Quayle misspelled the word "potatoe" and found egg on his face.

H. Ross Perot was the most serious third-party ticket in a very long time. His appeal crossed political boundaries. When the final votes were tallied, the renegade Texan had accumulated an impressive 19% of the popular vote.

President Bush and his team lost the general election in November to the brash young Arkansas Governor Bill Clinton and his running mate Senator Al Gore, Jr. "Yuppies" had taken over the White House; both newly elected officials were still in their forties.

SPORTS

The Chicago Bulls won the NBA championship for the second season in a row.

At the Olympics, the Dream Team of American basketball players beat all the competition. Included on the U.S. team were Patrick Ewing and the recently diagnosed HIV-positive Magic Johnson.

For the first time ever a Canadian team won the World Series, besting Atlanta in six games. At forty-one years old, Dave Winfield could still show his stuff.

TELEVISION

"Murphy Brown" returned to the air in the fall with a blistering attack on the vice president. At the Emmy Awards presentation, star Candice Bergen won for Best Actress in a comedy. She won laughs by thanking Quayle for bringing so much attention to her.

A Long Island scandal of epic proportions, the Amy Fisher saga, titillated Americans so much, that three, yes three, TV movies were made on the subject. As it was said, you'll never go broke underestimating the taste of the American public.

Also Notable: "Home Improvement," and Ken Burns's epic documentary "The Civil War," which made a star of historian Shelby Foote.

FADS AND FASHION

Marky Mark, the white rap singer, appeared in a series of ads for
Calvin Klein underwear. Mark popularized the dubious trend of
wearing pants on hips instead of at the waist.

1993

THE MOVIES

Jurassic Park directed by Steven Spielberg. Based on the hot book by Michael Crichton, director Spielberg was a master-technician when it came to special effects. (Note: *Jaws, Close Encounters of the Third Kind,* and *E. T.*) The tricks here were terrific, but the violence was the big problem. As with much of the Spielberg canon, there was merchandising money to be made. The advertising and promotional materials were aimed at very young children. But very young children would be too frightened to see this movie. What was the director thinking about? His audience or his wallet? Interestingly, Spielberg admitted that his young son Max would not be allowed to attend the film.

In the Line of Fire directed by Wolfgang Petersen. The man who created the very tense *Das Boot* was back at the helm. Clint Eastwood played a secret service agent haunted by the past; he failed to act the day John Kennedy was killed. Eastwood was consumed by his human failings. Now, yet another mental case was after another (fictional) president, and Eastwood had to prove himself and save the chief executive. John Malkovich, noted for his over-the-top performances, gave one of the best of his career. The secret service actually participated in the making of this movie which must have lent credibility. This movie, along with *JFK,* and *Love Field,* were a part of a small industry: the Kennedy death movies.

Short Cuts directed by Robert Altman. The short stories of Raymond Carver focused on the drab and the seemingly ordinary lives. Director Altman coaxed some of the finest actors to peak performances. The cast included Lily Tomlin, Jack Lemmon, and Tom Waits.

Also Notable: the presidential comedy *Dave* with Kevin Kline and Sigourney Weaver; *What's Love Got to Do with It?* the biopic of Tina Turner; and *Indecent Proposal,* with Robert Redford, Demi Moore, and Woody Harrelson, posing the question, "Would you sleep with Robert Redford for a million dollars?"

THE PLAYERS

Whoopi Goldberg scored big in 1992's *Sister Act* and followed that success with *Made in America* with her beau Ted Danson. Goldberg single-handedly gave new definition to the word "crossover." Everybody loved Whoopi.

Angela Bassett had her work cut out for her when she made *What's Love Got to Do with It?* She was playing the uniquely talented Tina Turner.

Emma Thompson and husband Kenneth Branagh were their generation's Laurence Olivier and Vivien Leigh. Their collaborations always meant class, such as their *Much Ado About Nothing.* How many people in 1993 Hollywood would tackle Shakespeare?

MUSIC

Pete Townshend was one of rock's wild men. It amazed many when, after winning a Tony Award for his *Tommy,* the former Who guitarist sang with the assembled theatre professionals. The song they belted out was the ultimate showstopper, Rodgers and Hammerstein's "Oklahoma!" Townshend's solo album hit it big. Its name: *PsychoDerelict.*

Janet Jackson's album *Janet* dominated the charts. She wasn't the phenomenon her brother was (Who is besides Madonna?) but she had a solid impact on the business. Her acting in the year's *Poetic Justice* expanded her horizons.

The Spin Doctors had a longtime hit album, *Pocket Full of Kryptonite*, which was super, man.

Also Notable: Rod Stewart's aping of Eric Clapton, with his *Unplugged* album; Gloria Estefan's *Mi Tierra*, broadened her non-Latin base with crossover hits; Tears for Fears attempted a come-back with *Elemental*.

Michael Jackson was the center of a child-molestation storm after being accused by a 13-year old boy. Jackson, on his world tour, checked into a clinic for drug rehabilitation.

LITERATURE

Just This Once by Scott French was really written by HAL. No, not the HAL from *2001,* but a computer just the same. French programmed the computer to write like the mistress of trash, Jacqueline Susann. The off-color writing made real writers see red.

The Last Brother by Joe McGinnis was a textbook case in how not to write a biography. In this case, McGinnis went after Edward M. Kennedy. The writer was no Truman Capote, and this was no *In Cold Blood.* Facts were derived from "other sources" and emotions and conversations were made-up. He should have just called it Kennedy-inspired fiction like so many other writers had. Those included Dominick Dunne and Joyce Carol Oates.

Radio shock-jock Howard Stern had his revenge-of-the-nerd when his book *Private Parts* soared to the top of the bestseller lists.

IN THE NEWS

On January 20, Bill Clinton was inaugurated as the forty-second president. Not since the mid-1800s had there been so many American presidents alive at one time: Nixon, Ford, Carter, Reagan, Bush, and Clinton. The new chief executive was a very young man who had high ideals even as a youth. He had protested the Vietnam war and did not serve. His eagerness to please caused him no end of trouble. He courted each side for a compromise, never standing firm with his own position.

One of the first tests before the president was allowing gays into the military. As a campaigner he was able to promise anything. As president he had to deal with the Congress, the Joint Chiefs of Staff, and public opinion.

In June it was discovered that, in California, a group of skinheads had plotted to set off a race war, reminiscent of Charles Manson's crazy plans.

The World Trade Center was bombed, leaving thousands dead or injured.

In July heavy rains hit the Midwest, creating floods and damage estimated at over $10 billion.

DRUGS

Talented young actor River Phoenix, known for his clean-living ways, died on a street outside The Viper Club in Los Angeles. Autopsy reports claimed he had died of a lethal combination of heroin and cocaine, commonly called a speed-ball.

SPORTS

The Chicago Bulls beat the Phoenix Suns, their third NBA championship in a row. This was the first time any team had "three-peated."

Every time Nolan Ryan struck out a batter he was breaking his own strike-out record. Ryan was approaching six thousand career strike-outs.

In Super Bowl play, the Washington Redskins bested the Buffalo Bills, 37–24.

TELEVISION

"Seinfeld" had been on the air for several seasons, but in 1993 the show took off. Starring stand-up comic Jerry Seinfeld, the program had a definite New York feel with situations and characters verging on neuroses and reality. In the show the characters pitched an idea to NBC about a stand-up comic and his friends. The show within a show would be about "nothing." Very Pirendellian, very funny.

David Letterman left his NBC late-night slot. It was rumored the funnyman was upset with the network because he had been passed over to replace Johnny Carson. Jay Leno got that slot. Letterman signed on with CBS, who bought the old Ed Sullivan Theatre especially for him. Now Letterman and Leno would go head-to-head.

Chevy Chase joined Arsenio Hall, Conan O'Brien, Leno, and Letterman in the late-night talk-show wars. Chase was the first casualty; his talk fest was cancelled after a few weeks. Fox replaced him with reruns of "In Living Color."

FADS AND FASHION

"Beavis & Butt-head" were animated MTV characters that were so obnoxious that many groups around the country protested their early-evening broadcasts. Their anti-social behavior, it was claimed, led to real-life arson cases.

1994

THE MOVIES

Pulp Fiction directed by Quentin Tarantino exploded onto the screen with its depiction of gruesome violence, drug use, and something else that separated it from other similar-themed films: a mosaic narrative. Actually several stories of corruption and crime rolled into one, Tarantino's dark film caught the attention of critics and the public, amassing over 100 million dollars at the box office. It catapulted John Travolta's career into high gear, after several years in neutral. Travolta, who was joined on screen by Samuel L. Jackson, Uma Thurman, Christopher Walken, Ving Rhames and Bruce Willis, went on to earn an Oscar nomination. Brutal and bloody, *Pulp Fiction* lifted America's acceptance of violence to a new high.

Forrest Gump was the movie everybody loved. It seemed like it would never leave the multiplex. As with many blockbusters, repeat customers helped propel the story of a "slow" Southern man into one of Hollywood's biggest money-makers of all time. Tom Hanks copped his second Academy Award in as many years and landed at the top of the very short list of stars whom everyone wanted to work with. Directed by one-time Steven Spielberg protégé, Robert Zemeckis, the movie featured great special effects, wherein historical figures interacted with movie characters. "There's Forrest Gump shaking hands with President Kennedy. How'd they do that?" Movie magic explains it.

The British are coming! *Four Weddings and a Funeral*, starring Hugh Grant, proved that the British film industry had a second home in America's heartland. After several years of stately films from such august concerns as Merchant/Ivory productions, Americans were used to "stiff-upper-lip" English movies. *Four Weddings* was a racy, laugh-filled romp that had everybody smiling.

Also Notable: America stayed away from Robert Redford's recreation of the 1950's scandals depicted in *Quiz Show*. Superbly acted and directed, the film demonstrated that the movie-going audience wasn't interested in anything so heady.

THE PLAYERS

With *Forrest Gump,* Tom Hanks became the closest thing to an American male "sweetheart" since the early days of James Stewart. Hanks was a great actor and a great star who could draw large numbers at the box office. Besides that, he seemed like everyone's friendly neighbor.

Shock jock Howard Stern attempted to run for governor of New York on the Libertarian Party ticket. Needless to say, he lost.

MUSIC

The grunge rock scene had taken off. The most notable purveyors were the Seattle-based group Nirvana. Lead singer Kurt Cobain, married to rocker Courtney Love of the band Hole, was the idol of legions of fans. Cobain's drug use was noted everywhere in the press. On April 5, Cobain shot himself in the head. As with other stars who die before their time, mystery and conspiracry theories surrounded the death. Cobain's ashes were scattered on a river in Washington State.

Bruce Springsteen's "Streets of Philadelphia" from the movie *Philadelphia* became a hit, won Springsteen an Oscar, and stood as a testament against intolerance.

Tony Bennett was rediscovered by the MTV generation. He won
the Grammy for Best Album of the year.

LITERATURE

Midnight in the Garden of Good and Evil by journalist John
Berendt read like a novel but was actually a recounting of a real-
life murder mystery in Savannah, Georgia. The plot had everything
necessary to keep it on the top of the bestseller lists for over a year.
It had sex, money, transvestites, high and low culture, and the
unique setting of genteel Savannah, a city that woke up from its
sleepy slumber to find itself inundated with tourists who wanted to
journey the paths made famous in the book.

The Alienist by Caleb Carr was an eerie evocation of the grime and
crime in NewYork City during the turn of the century. A page-
turning mystery, it was also a slice of historical recreation.

IN THE NEWS

Former President Richard M. Nixon, who resigned from office in
1974, died in New York City on April 22 after suffering a stroke. In
his later years, Nixon had tried and succeeded in rehabilitating his
name and reputation and was considerred an elder statesman, having revisited China and the former Soviet Union. However, his enemies, real and imagined, would never let go of the image of Nixon
as corrupt and evil. Nixon was buried at the Nixon Library next to
his wife Pat, who died in 1993. Democrat President Bill Clinton
gave the eulogy. Clinton's wife, Hillary, had been a staff attorney
during the Senate Watergate hearings.

During one of Nixon's last hospitals stays, it would be noted ironically, that in the same facility at the same time was Jacqueline
Kennedy Onassis also in her final days.

On May 19, the former queen of Camelot, "Jackie" to her many
fans and admirers, died in her home in New York City. Jackie had

been the closest thing America had to being real royalty. She had style, bearing, and the good fortune to have incredible wealth to make it all look easy. In many ways, all roads led to Jackie. There'd never been one like her in the media's eye or in history. Like Nixon's funeral, Jackie's was given national press attention as she was laid to rest next to her husband, President John F. Kennedy, at Arlington National Cemetery in Virginia. Again, John F. Kennedy, Jr., was a memorable sight at the funeral of one of his parents. He and his sister Caroline demostrated their brave reserve in the face of tragedy.

As First Lady, Jackie had held a nation's hand during one of its most fragile moments. As a world celebrity, her every move was monitored by the press. Always aware of her place in history, her public persona never interfered with her role as mother and grand-mother. No other First Lady, with the exception of Eleanor Roosevelt, had such a lasting impact on the American psyche. However, even in her last days, as thousands stood in vigil outside her New York apartment building, there were those who scorned Jackie as a mere "social climber" without "class."

SPORTS

The Nancy Kerrigan-Tonya Harding affair continued to engross the population hungry for a real-life melodrama. Had Harding hired someone to crack the knees of her rival ice-skater Kerrigan? Was Nancy too good and pure to capture American sympathy? Would the press ever back off?

Basketball superstar Michael Jordan left the game to pursue his childhood dream of being a baseball player.

Woodstock '94. On the 25th anniversary of the biggest rock festi-val ever, thousands again congregated in upstate New York. Bob Dylan played, and so did younger acts like Nine Inch Nails.

TELEVISION

Two hospital-based dramas debuted. "ER" aired on NBC, while "Chicago Hope" was on CBS. From the start, "ER" was the more successful with a cast that included George Clooney, Noah Wyle, Anthony Edwards and Julianna Margulies. Margulies was billed as a guest star on the first episode—her character was supposed to be brain-dead from a suicide attempt. In a strange twist in television history, George Clooney had been a regular on a situation comedy ten years earlier, also entitled, "E/R."

ARREST AND TRIAL (PART I)

Sometime before midnight on June 12, Nicole Brown Simpson and her friend Ronald Goldman are murdered in Brentwood, California. O. J. Simpson, the former football player and movie star, flies to Chicago. The news breaks that blood stains found in O. J. Simpson's vehicle and in his driveway match those found at the crime scene, the home of his former wife. Nicole Simpson and Ronald Goldman were found to be the victims of sharp force injures, deep knife wounds. In fact, Nicole's head was nearly removed through the force of her injuries. On June 17, O. J. Simpson is charged with two counts of murder. He does not surrender but remains at-large. He is declared a fugitive. A white Ford Bronco, owned by Simpson pal Al Cowlings, is spotted by Los Angeles police on an expressway. Simpson and Cowlings lead the police on a 60-mile low-speed pursuit that is broadcast on national television. He is arrested and jailed without bail. This was the beginning of what many people have called "the trial of the century," displacing the Lindbergh baby kidnapping from that notorious place in the annals of crime. The arrest and trial of O. J. Simpson opened wounds along racial and social lines, created questions about justice American-style, and became an industry in and of itself, lifting many unfamiliar faces out of obscurity and onto the front pages of newspapers and magazines. Book and movie deals emerged, millions of dollars exchanged hands, careers were made, while the entire nation sat glued to their television sets waiting to hear the next little detail of these two gruesome murders. Who had heard of Johnnie Cochran, Robert Shapiro, Marcia Clark, or Christopher Darden? Before the end of it all, each would become famous and rich, if not richer for their involvement in this crime.

1995

THE MOVIES

One of the weakest years for American movies since the dawn of talkies, 1995 will be remembered as the year that foisted *Braveheart* on an unsuspecting public. Released in the summer to grab the attention of teenagers, it unexpectantly garnered praise from the *New York Times* critic Janet Maslin, who must have confused the film's high cost with high quality. Her glowing review didn't help at the box office, but the filmmakers, including director/star Mel Gibson, didn't let that stop them. They rereleased the film in the fall, again to wide yawns. Whenever someone says there isn't magic in the movies anymore, all one has to do is point out *Braveheart*. Someone must have cast a spell on the Academy of Motion Picture Arts and Sciences. There is no other explanation why this depressing downer of a movie won Best Picture.

Thrillers are supposed to catch an audience off guard, fill them with suspense and otherwise entertainingly shock. *The Usual Suspects* delivered in every department. With a great cast that included Kevin Spacey in an amazing performance, the film was a real triumph for screenwriter Christopher McQuarrie.

Not since Arnold Ziffel from the 1960's sitcom "Green Acres" has a talking pig gone so far in show business. *Babe* was a favorite from the barnyard to the schoolyard with its kinda-corny, screwed-up tale of a cunning little piglet.

Nixon managed to celebrate and denounce the country's 37th president all at the same time. What else could be expected from director Oliver Stone? His diatribe against Nixon inadvertantly showed the vulnerable side of the former president, making him sympathetic. Most of the credit went to Anthony Hopkins, who turned in an extraordinary performance as Nixon the man.

Also Notable: *Toy Story*. This animated movie featured the voices of Tom Hanks and Tim Allen as rival toys, what else? This was another sort of crossover movie. Even parents liked to play with *Toy Story*.

THE PLAYERS

It's good to have relatives in the business. Just ask Oscar-winner Nicolas Cage, who took home his award for *Leaving Las Vegas*. The nephew of director Francis Ford Coppola would probably still be waiting on tables in a diner in Van Nuys if not for his famous relative. In Hollywood, however, it's all about family, sometimes just like the Corleone family.

Emma Thompson, an also-ran for Best Actress for *Sense and Sensibility*, does not go home empty-handed. She becomes the first Best Actress (*Howards End*) to also win an Academy Award for best screenplay of the Jane Austen classic. The film itself sets off a veritable Jane Austen retrospective with feature films and television shows based on the English writer's works.

MUSIC

Alanis Morissette won multiple Grammys. Her "Jagged Little Pill" won Album of the Year and Best Rock Album. "You Oughta Know" won Best Rock Song and Best Female Rock Vocal Performance. Her spiteful and bileful delivery enabled her to break away from the pack of similar-sounding, edgy female artists like Sinead O'Connor and Siouxsie Sioux.

Selena, billed as the "Tex-Mex Madonna," had won the Tejano Music Award for Best Female Performer and was about to become a major crossover artist. Instead, she was murdered on March 31 by Yolanda Saldivar, a woman who ran her fan club.

IN THE NEWS

On April 19, on the second anniversary of the standoff at Waco, Texas, between the cult Branch Davidians and the Alcohol, Tobacco and Firearms authorities, the Alfred P. Murrah Federal Building in Oklahoma City, Oklahoma was bombed, leaving 168 people, including many children dead. Many others were seriously injured. Initial reaction was that there were foreign terrorists in the heartland of America. But the actual perpetrators, Timothy McVeigh and Terry Nichols, were home-grown terrorists.

On June 27, Hugh Grant, popular star of *Sense and Sensibility* and *Four Weddings and a Funeral* was arrested in Hollywood and booked on suspicion of lewd conduct after he was caught having oral sex with a prostitute, Divine Brown. Grant's relationship with model/actress Elizabeth Hurley teetered on the verge of extinction. Grant's new film *Nine Months* opened shortly after to big office success, proving that there is no such thing as bad press. When Grant appeared on "The Tonight Show with Jay Leno" on July 24, the NBC show won the weekly ratings race with David Letterman.

SPORTS

Olympic diver Greg Louganis disclosed that he was gay and HIV+. Almost immediately, concern sprang up that when Louganis made his famous fall several years before, his blood had tainted the pool water. His disclosure helped sales of his book.

Michael Jordan returned to basketball after his brief fling as a baseball player with the Chicago White Sox.

Dennis Rodman, Michael Jordan and Scottie Pippin became an unstoppable triumvirate with the Chicago Bulls. The team won 72 games during the regular season.

Mickey Mantle, the Yankee great, died. The hero of a generation of baseball fans, the "Mick" lived a life far different from a storybook dream. His wild drinking ways led him to have a liver transplant. Mickey Mantle was a hero to his fans, but a much more complicated man to those who knew him. It had once been reported that on any given day, Mantle would be able to name only three of his four children.

TELEVISION

"The Gary Shandling Show" debuted on Comedy Central. The show-within-a-show became a favorite of those literate enough to understand the host's loopy humor.

Michael Jackson, the King of Pop, and his wife Lisa-Marie Presley, the daughter of the King Elvis, appeared together on the air to discuss their private lives. It was a royal pain.

NBC's Thursday night line-up of comedies punctuated by the ten o'clock drama "ER" continued to be a major draw.

ARREST AND TRIAL (PART II)

On October 3, flanked by defense attorney Johnnie Cochran and longtime friend Robert Kardashion, O. J. Simpson was aquitted in the brutal stabbing murders of his ex-wife Nicole and her friend Ron Goldman. Simpson family members cried with joy as the relatives of Goldman wept in anguish. Testimony had taken nine months with 120 witnesses, 45,000 pages of evidence and over 1,000 exhibits. The jury of 10 women and 2 men, comprised of nine blacks, two whites and one Hispanic, took less than four hours to reach a verdict. Until the verdict was read, the general feeling was that the decision could go either way. Goldman's family promised to sue Simpson in a civil wrongful death case.

FADS AND FASHION

Mr. Potato Head makes a comeback. Yes, he'd been gone for nearly three decades, but with the release of *Toy Story,* the tater head was back as a popular toy. A chip off the old block.

IT ISN'T JUST A FAD

Personal computers became part of millions of households. Access to the World Wide Web introduced new words like "cyberspace," "downloading," and oh, yes, "the Internet." The world became a much smaller place. "I'll e-mail you" meant that someone in Costa Rica didn't have to pick up the telephone and call long-distance if they wanted to share a few minutes with a friend in New York. Junk mail now came with your postal delivery and your e-mail. There were no more excuses about telephones being busy because you could always leave an e-mail. Along with the introduction of the Internet, came "chat rooms" and other forms of interaction, all of which meant that no one ever had to leave home. Ever. You wanted to buy something, go on the Net and buy it from one of those start-up companies such as Amazon or eToys. Start-up companies? What are they? An explosion of technologies spreads through the country, making instant millionaires and billionaires out of "computer geeks." The stock market grows to include not only traditional businesses, or Old Economies, but new technologies, the New Economy.

1996

THE MOVIES

Fargo. You'd have to travel a long distance to find a movie as engaging, subversive, and twisted as this Joel Coen–directed slice of Midwest life. In fact Joel and brother/writing partner Ethan had already built a steady career with offbeat movies like *Blood Simple, Raising Arizona* and *Barton Fink,* but this was by far the most successful and accessible. Frances McDormand, Mrs. Coen in real life, starred as a pregnant sheriff out to find a killer. Perverse in every good sense of the word, *Fargo* had audiences laughing at the same time they were questioning their mirth. A career high for the Coen brothers, the movie also introduced to a wide audience the very peculiar talents of Steve Buscemi, a man whose face you won't—and shouldn't—soon forget.

Jerry Maguire proved once and for all that Tom Cruise could act, given the right role and right director. Cameron Crowe not only directed but wrote the screenplay for this very appealing look at the life of the title character, a sports agent-turned-man. The actress with the unlikely name of Renee Zellweger costarred as his weepy but nice love interest. The show was stolen, however, by Cuba Gooding Jr.'s Rod Tidwell, the only athlete left on Maguire's roster of talent once he's fired from his big-time agency. "Show me the money," was Tidwell's plea to Maguire and it caught on across the country. Bosses soon heard employees exclaim, "Show me the money!" Hollywood needn't have worried. The cash rolled in for this box-office champ. However, the disarming fact remained:

Jerry Maguire was the only studio-produced film that made it into the final five Best Picture nominees. Hollywood, long out of touch with what was popular, continued to make blaring special-effect films. The independent production companies, most notably Miramax, showed the big boys a thing or two by scrambling harder for theaters and by signing interesting players to interesting projects.

Also Notable: *Evita* starring Madonna was a box-office dud, but even with the star's limited acting range, the movie proved potent. It also proved that Antonio Banderas was more than just a pretty face. *The People vs. Larry Flynt*, directed by Milos Forman, made an unlikely hero out of "Hustler" publisher Flynt, and made an unlikely star out of Woody Harrelson.

THE PLAYERS

After 50 years in the business, it looked like Lauren Bacall would finally take home an Oscar. The veteran star (her name was included in the lyrics to *Evita*) was up for Best Supporting Actress in the Barbra Streisand–directed *The Mirror Has Two Faces,* but lost to the incredibly beautiful Juliette Binoche for her pivotal role in *The English Patient.*

James Woods turned ugly and racist for his role in *Ghosts of Mississippi*, based on the true story of a Ku Klux Klan member averting trial for murder.

Adam Sandler wasn't likely to win any acting awards but he did prove himself a box-office winner and the heir to Jerry Lewis's manic type of humor. After 1995's *Billy Madison*, Sandler was back with the equally nutty *Happy Gilmore*. Hollywood had to notice and they did. Sandler was signed to a multi-million dollar contract. The list of "Saturday Night Live" stars to cross into films got longer: Chevy Chase, Dan Ackroyd, John Belushi, Gilda Radner, Eddie Murphy, Dana Carvey, Chris Farley, and now Sandler.

MUSIC

The Grammy for Record of the Year went to rock legend Eric Clapton for his "Change the World."

Beck won Best Male Vocal of the Year for "Where It's At."

Mariah Carey and Boyz II Men have a hit with "One Sweet Day."

In August, "The Macarena" hit the airwaves, dance clubs and wedding receptions like the *Titanic* hitting that iceberg. Everybody was humming along to the catchy Latin beat made popular by Los del Rio. Even Vice President Al Gore, famously stiff and ill-at ease, had some fun with the song during the summer Democratic Convention.

People were also listening to the hot soundtrack to the surprise hit movie, *Waiting to Exhale.* It didn't hurt that Whitney Houston was on the recording.

Madonna's latest release was her first child, Lourdes.

LITERATURE

The power of daytime television's Oprah Winfrey grew to new heights. She initiated the Oprah Book Club. The first selection was Jacquelyn Mitchard's *The Deep End of the Ocean*, a woman's book to be sure. Month after month, "Oprah's picks," as they are called, made it to the prestigious *New York Times* bestseller list, making instant millionaires of sometimes obscure authors. From the time Oprah instituted her book club, she became a major force in the book industry. Her empire continued to grow in many directions, all of them successful. Oprah's take was simple: make it spirtual and make it real.

Basketball star Dennis Rodman published his autobiography *Bad As I Wanna Be,* in which he disclosed his penchant for wearing women's clothing for fun. Rodman became a media sensation, which is not saying he didn't become a media whore.

IN THE NEWS

On July 17, a Boeing 747 out of New York's JFK airport in flight to Paris, carrying 230 passengers and crew members, exploded and crashed for no apparent reason off the coast of Long Island. TWA Flight 800 was shrouded in mystery and conspiracy theories. Had the U.S. Navy inadvertantly shot down the plane? Was terrorist Osama bin Laden responsible? No matter what the reason, there was no answer to the puzzling question of why. The question remains unsatisfactorily answered to this day.

Incumbents Bill Clinton and Al Gore handily defeated Republican challengers Bob Dole and Jack Kemp to retain the White House. Dole, in a daring move, had resigned from the Senate and thus his powerful leadership position, in order to devote himself full-time to his presidential run. It didn't pay off.

On Thursday, December 26, JonBenet Ramsey of Boulder, Colorado, was found murdered in her family's three-story mansion. She was all of 6-years-old. Born in Atlanta to John and Patricia Ramsey, JonBenet sparkled as a contestant in beauty pageants, but her real claim to fame was the mystery that surrounded her death. A ransom note was left behind. Who wrote it? John or Patricia? Or someone else? An unknown intruder? But why would an unknown intruder take the time to leave a ransom note after he'd killed his victim? Nothing made sense in this senseless crime. JonBenet was 6-years-old, after all. What threat could she have posed to anyone? In cases like this, the parents are often thought of as the most likely suspects. But the case remains an eerie mystery with the indelible image of JonBenet's highly made-up face and grown-up clothes accentuating the surrealism of this all-too-real story.

SPORTS

In a first for a U.S. women's team, they took home the gold in gymnastics. Kerri Strug, 18 years old, led the team but had to be carried to the medal stand by her coach Bela Karolyi because of a foot injury.

TELEVISION

Talk show host Phil Donahue called it quits after 29 years of liberal-minded television chat.

"3rd Rock from the Sun" debuted on NBC. The comedy starred John Lithgow, Kristen Johnson, French Stewart, and Joseph Gordon-Levitt as space aliens who come to earth and live in Ohio. The slapstick humor and pratfalls ran opposed to the "cool" and "hip" urban comedies popular at the time. The cast would seemingly do anything for a laugh. NBC, thinking the show was somehow a lesser form of comedy, kept moving its timeslot. Fans had to find it and did so despite the network's best efforts.

Martha Stewart's empire takes hold. The queen of creative domesticity becomes a fixture on the television scene. Offering advice on everything from sewing to cooking to gardening, Martha replaces American grandmothers as the dispensaries of how to get things done the right way. Her "It's a good thing" phrase certainly works for her. Martha Stewart eventually becomes a billionaire.

Helen Hunt and Paul Reiser captivated audiences and their show, "Mad About You" continued on the air.

"Law & Order" was a continuing hit for NBC. The gritty stories set in New York were often taken right from the headlines.

1997

THE MOVIES

Forget *Gone with the Wind.* When *Titanic* sailed into theaters, it created a buzz like no other in film history since the Civil War epic of 1939. The film catapulted Leonardo DiCaprio into heartthrob status and ended up breaking box office records. It didn't start out that way, though. The trouble-plagued production was hinted to be a disaster in the making, running far over its original costs. Director James Cameron, of *Terminator* fame, was unbowed by pre-release criticism and was ultimately proven right in his adherance to period detail. Of course the sinking of the Titanic took longer in the film than it did in real life, but no one in the massive audience cared a whit about that. They were stunned by the visual effects. And rightfully so. *Titanic* appealed to everyone, even though the story was little more than a conventional rich girl/poor boy rehash. It worked big time. The film garnered a staggering 14 Academy Award nominations, tying *All About Eve* in that tally. It went on to win 11 Oscars, tying only *Ben Hur* for the most ever won. Cameron won Best Director, but was roundly, and justifiably, lampooned, when he accepted the award and uttered a line from the movie, "I'm King of the world." Well, maybe he was King of the Oscars, but a little bit of humility would have been a good thing. *Titanic* became the top-grossing film of all time, taking in over $600,000,000 in the United States and Canada alone.

L.A. Confidential was the sleeper that some malcontents thought would prevent *Titanic* from sweeping the major awards. It was not to be. A smart *film noir*, the type Hollywood used to crank out by the dozens, it caught audiences' attention by its gripping story. The terrific cast included two young Australian actors, Guy Pierce and Russell Crowe, along with James Cromwell, Kevin Spacey, and in her Oscar-winning performance, Kim Basinger.

As Good As It Gets was another trouble-plagued production that needed reshoots before its initial release. Rumors swirled around this James L. Brooks–directed production the same way they had around his previous bomb *I Love Trouble.* Jack Nicholson and Helen Hunt made an unusual couple, since Shirley Knight, who played Hunt's mother, was just about Nicholson's age. Hollywood superstar men like Warren Beatty, Robert Redford, and Harrison Ford, often costarred with women who could have been their daughters. The same would never hold true for Hollywood's female population. They don't get to have romantic leads half their age. Once they turn fifty, they play "the mother."

Austin Powers: International Man of Mystery was as lowbrow as movie comedies could get without losing its intention: just be funny. Mike Myers played the thawed-out 1960's spy now set loose in contemporary London. Costarring were Elizabeth Hurley and veteran Robert Wagner who played "Number Two." Wagner lampooned his sauve and sophisticated image with great results.

Also Notable: *Good Will Hunting*, starring Matt Damon and Ben Affleck. The two actors wrote the script and took home Oscars for it.

Boogie Nights might have sounded like a light comedy, but was anything but. The creepy goings-on in the L. A. porn world were the subject of this very disturbing flick. What it had going for it was a superior cast, headed by, of all people, Burt Reynolds, a man who finally proved himself to be a worthy actor.

THE PLAYERS

Leonardo DiCaprio had been nominated for Best Supporting Actor for his role in *What's Eating Gilbert Grape?* in 1993, but found superstar status playing Jack Dawson in the megahit *Titanic*. Not since the early days of John Travolta had an actor so consumed the female population. Nicknamed Leo, his every move was reported by the press. His group of friends were referred to as his "posse." The unrelenting eye of paparazzi spied on him, as it did his costar, Kate Winslet. However, Winslet wasn't apt to play the Hollywood game and soon went back to playing roles in arty British films. DiCaprio, the biggest star on the planet, looked for more commercial vehicles. What DiCaprio did not receive was Oscar consideration. He alone stood out as one member of the *Titanic* crew who did not get a nomination.

Gloria Stuart, an octogenarian who had been around since the early talkies, reclaimed part of the spotlight by playing the aged Kate Winslet in *Titanic*. It brought her an Oscar nomination and a place in the history books. At no other time had two actresses been nominated for Oscars for playing the same character in the same movie.

Jack Nicholson also made it into the record books. Being honored for his role in *As Good As It Gets* put him in very esteemed territory. Katharine Hepburn had four Oscars, all leads. Walter Brennan had three supporting awards. Ingrid Bergman had two as leading lady and one as a supporting cast member. Now Nicholson had two for leading roles and one for supporting.

Kim Basinger took home an Oscar for supporting actress in *L.A. Confidential*, but the awards seemed to be for lifetime achievement. She had overcome awful publicity, both personally and professionally, and this award put her on the map as a serious actress.

MUSIC

Titanic swamped the competition in this area, too. Celine Dion's heart-wrenching "My Heart Will Go On" proved to be an unsinkable hit. Musically, it derived inspiration from traditional Gaelic songs, in keeping with character Jack Dawson's background. Dion's lyrical voice perfectly fit the melancholy of the song.

The son also rises. Jakob Dylan, son of Bob, burst onto the music scene as lead singer of the group The Wallflowers. "One Headlight" became one of the hottest songs of the year.

Boy groups took over the airwaves. Groups such as The Backstreet Boys brought their generic, but soulful sounds to teenage girls ready for their first crush.

A mini British invasion occurs when the Spice Girls release their self-titled album. Everybody wanted a little bit more spice in their life.

LITERATURE

The Perfect Storm by Sebastian Junger took book buyers by storm. The true story of fishermen lost at sea during a massive weather disturbance reinvigorated non-fiction in American publishing. It started a trend of real-life adventures surging to the top of bestseller lists, such as *Into the Wild* and *Into Thin Air* (one of several about climbing Mount Everest), both by Jon Krakauer.

THIS ACTUALLY HAPPENED (PART I)

On July 15, international fashion designer Gianni Versace was shot in the back of the head on the steps of his luxurious South Beach, Florida, mansion. A gay serial killer, Andrew Cunanan, was the subject of a manhunt and was found dead of self-inflicted wounds on July 23. The killing was left without explanation. Attending Versace's funeral were his close friends Elton John and Princess Diana.

THIS ACTUALLY HAPPENED (PART II)

On August 31, Princess Diana and her boyfriend, millionaire play-boy Dodi al Fayed, were killed, along with their driver Henri Paul, in a car crash in Paris. The driver, found to be legally drunk after an autopsy was performed, had been driving the car at very high speeds through one of Paris' tunnels. Reports suggested that they were speeding to get away from the paparazzi who were following them. Elton John sang a rewritten version of his tribute to Marilyn Monroe, "Candle in the Wind," at Princess Diana's funeral.

THIS ACTUALLY HAPPENED (PART III)

Michael Kennedy, son of slain Senator Robert F. Kennedy, had been in the news for his alleged relationship with his children's babysitter. Michael's first cousin, John F. Kennedy Jr., editor of the magazine *George*, called Michael "the poster child for bad behav-ior." On December 31, Michael Kennedy was killed in a freak acci-dent as he played football on skis in Aspen, Colorado.

IN THE NEWS

On May 2, Los Angeles police arrested Eddie Murphy. He had of-fered a ride to a 21-year-old passenger because she "looked tired." However, on closer examination, the passenger turned out to be a transsexual prostitute.

On October 1, in Pearl, Mississippi, Luke Woodham, a 16-year-old gunman, went on a rampage, killing two students and injuring sev-eral others. Later in the day, it was discovered that the boy had also killed his own mother.

On December 1, in Paduccah, Kentucky, a 14-year-old freshman, Michael Carneal, went on a killing rampage. Carneal was inspired by the Leonardo DiCaprio movie *Basketball Diaries,* wherein there is a fantasy sequence of a young boy killing his classmates.

A British au pair, Louise Woodward, was convicted of second-degree murder of 8-month-old Matthew Eappen. Her sentence was reduced to time served after the judge reduced the charge to manslaughter.

SPORTS

On December 2, Oakland Warriors' Latrell Sprewell was suspended indefinitely for what the team said was an attack on his coach, P. J. Carlesimo. The star guard reportedly threatened to kill Carlesimo during practice.

Mike Tyson was banned from boxing after biting off part of heavyweight champion Evander Holyfield's ear during a bout. That sent Tyson for a loop.

TELEVISION

"Ally McBeal" starred Calista Flockhart as a young attorney making her way through the legal profession as well as through her own romantic insecurities. It gave young American women a fairly honest role model. Its sometimes bizarre plot interruptions gave the show a fresh look. It wasn't only women who tuned in and made this a big hit.

"The Practice" opened for business on ABC. Set in Boston, this was a brainy legal show from creator David E. Kelley, who was responsible for the Fox hit "Ally McBeal." Starring Dylan McDermott, Lara Flynn Boyle, and Camryn Manheim, it featured twisty plots, intelligent performers and inspired casting. It gave people plenty of reason to hurry home to tune in on Sunday nights. So-called "stunt" programming sometimes had "Ally McBeal" and "The Practice" have interrelated story lines. Only a producer as powerful as Kelley could convince two different networks to do something as interesting as this.

After months of teasing the public, "Ellen" star Ellen DeGeneres comes out as a lesbian both on air and in real life. Her love interest on her series was played by Laura Dern. In real life, DeGeneres made a sensation by hooking up with actress Anne Heche, formerly romantically linked to comic/writer Steve Martin. Heche apparently liked people who were funny.

On August 13, "South Park" debuted. Created by Trey Parker and Matt Stone, the show pushed the envelope of bad taste, even by the standards of cable.

FADS AND FASHION

Violent video games swept the nation. Mortal Kombat was among the top sellers.

1998

THE MOVIES

It was war, not just between the Allies and the Axis Powers but between Dreamworks and Miramax. Both studios had major releases in 1998, each vying for audiences and awards. Unlike the outcome of World War II, this one led to a split decision.

Saving Private Ryan (Dreamworks) was director Steven Spielberg's acclaimed and disturbing second foray into the World War II arena, after his triumph with *Schindler's List.* Starring Tom Hanks, again as Everyman, the movie was a startling re-creation of what war was about. The first 45 minutes of the film were as seemingly real as any documentary. Costarring with Hanks was hot newcomer Matt Damon and Ed Burns. Much of the movie featured plot machinations right out of World War II flicks of the 1940s, however, and instead of ringing true-to-life like its opening sequence, the film faltered at the end. The result was disappointing. Audiences felt they'd seen another "Spielberg" movie, that is, sentimental and emotionally exhausting, instead of a reasoned, mature view of war. However, Spielberg took home his second Academy Award for directing.

Shakespeare in Love, from a screenplay by Marc Norman and playwright Tom Stoppard, was Miramax's contribution to the battle. Adult, educated audiences loved the movie which depicted a young Will Shakespeare in the throes of his first love affair. Joseph

Fiennes and Gwyneth Paltrow portrayed the lovers. It was dreamy, humorous and just what the Academy thinks of as "art." It took home the Best Picture.

Also Notable: Terence Malick's first film in many years, *The Thin Red Line*, was another contemplation of America's involvement in World War II. This was set in the Pacific, as opposed to *Private Ryan*, which was set in Europe.

Americans weren't alone in looking back at the war. Italian Roberto Benigni wrote, directed and starred in *Life Is Beautiful*, a unique entry in the canon of World War II movies.

The Truman Show was directed by Peter Weir as a star vehicle for Jim Carrey. Carrey wanted desperately to be taken seriously as an actor and every frame of this film showed him working to that end.

There's Something About Mary went as far as any mainstream American film ever did in its depiction of body fluids. Directed by brothers Bobby and Peter Farrelly, it starred Cameron Diaz, Matt Dillon, and Ben Stiller. They got themselves out of some very sticky situations.

Armageddon starred Bruce Willis and Liv Tyler. It told the story of the end of the world, but it racked up so much money the producers would have been easily able to buy another world.

THE PLAYERS

During the 1950s, big stars like Clark Gable would mangle the foreign names of the actors, writers and directors as they read the nominees for Oscars. In a "polictically correct" world of 1998, this behavior would seem offensive. In steps Roberto Benigni. His antics on various award shows, and most especially on the Oscars, demonstrated a throwback to "bumbling Italians" who mangled English that was just as insulting as Gable ever was.

The golden girl of many a Miramax film (read: low-budget) was Gwyneth Paltrow. When she accepted her Oscar for Best Actress she proved that she continually acted on and off screen. Her teary, overly theatrical thanks to her father seemed well rehearsed.

MUSIC

He had been called The Chairman of the Board, The Voice, Old Blues Eyes, among many other phrases. No matter what anyone thought of his personal life, Frank Sinatra had been the focal point of mass media attention for most of his professional career. He had been the quintessential bobbysoxer idol (precursor to the teen heartthrob), recording artist, movie star, stage presence, mogul, presidential pal, and power broker. He was also known for his mob connections. He had left his childhood sweetheart to marry one of the world's most beautiful women, Ava Gardner. He married 19-year-old Mia Farrow when he was in his forties. His widow was Barbara Marx. Along the way he was romantically linked with Lauren Bacall and Juliette Prowse, among many others, some unknowns, even to him. On May 14, at the age of 83, Frank Sinatra died.

"I Don't Want to Miss a Thing" by Aerosmith was a blockbuster hit, but when it was performed on the Oscar telecast (it was nominated for Best Song), it appeared that lead singer Steve Tyler was singing a love song to the images of his daughter Liv, who appeared in the film *Armageddon*.

"The Boy is Mine," a duet by Brandy and Monica, soared to the number-one position on the charts.

"Candle in the Wind," Elton John's elegy to Princess Diana, became one of the best-selling singles in the world.

Country singer LeAnn Rimes belted out a hit with "How Do I Live." And she was just a teenager.

LITERATURE

The British are coming! The British are here! English author J. K. Rowling made publishing history with her Harry Potter books. Children and adults alike ate up the stories of a boy wizard, his Cinderlad childhood, and his adventures at Hogwarts School of Witchcraft and Wizardry. Critically acclaimed, the series continues to find new readers with each installment.

IN THE NEWS

Rivaling only the Watergate affair of the 1970s, the Bill Clinton affair at least had sex involved instead of merely an unnamed Deep Throat. On January 21, Independent Counsel, Kenneth Starr, who was looking into the matter of Bill Clinton's uninvited sexual advances on one Paula Jones, reported that President Bill Clinton urged a former White House intern to deny that they had an affair. The next day the president denied the allegations. Hillary Clinton went on the "Today" show in support of her husband, saying that he was a target of "a vast right-wing conspiracy." By now, everyone had a conspiracy theory about something. The immaculately coiffed First Lady didn't look so good when the truth came out that the president had, in fact, had a relationship with the intern. Knowing that she would go down in history [sic], Monica Lewinsky, the former intern, kept incriminating evidence, such as a stained blue dress. Why anyone would keep a stained garment, except with the foreknowledge that it would be used as evidence, was never explained. Lewinsky's name itself became a verb for a sexual act. Lewinsky's former friend, Linda Tripp, a disgruntled government employee, was willing to turn in her friend in exchange for a book contract. However, when that never materialized, Tripp turned ugly. Pleading on television that she was like any other good American, Linda Tripp never thought that most good Americans wouldn't tape conversations with their friends for later use against them. Millions of dollars were spent investigating the president and his shenanigans. But since the economy was running at an all-time high, most people didn't see the need to draw blood from the Man from

Hope. Senate Republicans saw it differently and urged impeachment.

On April 7, Los Angeles detective Marcelo Rodriquez arrested singer George Michael for lewd behavior in a public bathroom at Will Rogers Memorial Park in Beverly Hills. Not only did this mark Michael's fall from grace, but his public "outing" as being gay.

THIS ACTUALLY HAPPENED (PART IV)

On January 5, less than a week after the bizarre death of Michael Kennedy in a skiing accident, singer-turned-politician Sonny Bono died in a skiing mishap as well. Two freakish deaths within one week. At Congressman Bono's funeral, his former wife, Cher, took center stage and wept as she recalled their life together, ignoring the fact that they had publicly fueded and that Sonny left a widow, Mary. The widow Bono, in turn, grabbing the spotlight herself, accepted the Congressional seat left open by the death of her husband. The only person who seemed in the least bit normal was Sonny and Cher's lesbian daughter Chastity.

SPORTS

On January 23, Superbowl XXXII became one of the highest-rated sports broadcasts ever. Considered one of the best face-offs in the history of Superbowls, the Denver Broncos were led to victory over the Green Bay Packers by 37-year-old quarterback, John Elway.

Move over Mantle and Maris, here come McGwire and Sosa. Not since the heated homerun race of 1961 did two heavy hitters capture the public's imagination. First baseman for the St. Louis Cardinals, number 25, Mark McGwire, and Chicago Cubs outfielder, number 21, Sammy Sosa, took swing after swing for the record books. Instead of the intense rivalry of Maris and Mantle, however, Sosa and McGwire genuinely seemed to like each other.

By the end of the year, both had topped the Maris record of 61 homeruns. McGwire finished the year with 70 and Sosa with 66.

"Baywatch" beauty Carmen Electra married basketball and media star Dennis Rodman. The marriage lasted all of six months.

TELEVISION

"Sex and the City" premiered on HBO on June 6. The lusty stories of four sexually active New York single women were refreshingly different from the tittering and titillating prattle that doomed many network series. It brought well-deserved stardom to Sarah Jessica Parker, Kim Cattrall, Kristin Davis, and Cynthia Nixon.

"Will and Grace" debuted on NBC. For the first time an openly gay man was the lead character of a sitcom. Gay Will, along with his straight friend Grace, were only two parts of a quartet of actors who kept the show very funny. The four were: Eric McCormack, Debra Messing, Megan Mullaly, and Sean Hayes.

FADS AND FASHION

Japanese-created Pokemon swept the imaginations of children throughout America. With toys, games, cards, stick-ons, and eventually movies, Pokemon reigned.

1999

THE MOVIES

The American movie industry had one of its best years in quite a while. There was a wide variety of high-quality films to choose from. Finally.

American Beauty owed a lot to 1960's *The Apartment*. Both were cynical reflections on how the American culture wasn't all that it seemed to be on the very pretty surface. Not far beneath the sheen of success was disillusionment, disappointment, and disaster. In the last analysis, *American Beauty* went further than its predecessor, killing off its hero. The success of first-time filmmaker Sam Mendes was even more notable since he was a British theatrical director prior to this. Star Kevin Spacey openly acknowledged *The Apartment*'s director Billy Wilder in his Oscar acceptance speech. Spacey could have mentioned as well Wilder's *Sunset Boulevard*, another influence on *American Beauty*. After all, how many films are narrated by dead men? Joining Spacey was a remarkable cast that included Annette Bening, Peter Gallagher, Mena Suvari, and Chris Cooper.

The Sixth Sense. Who would have wanted to go see a movie with Bruce Willis and an unknown kid named Haley Joel Osment? It was spooky how many people decided that this was their favorite movie of the year and went to see it twice. The fact of the matter was the movie was so cleverly constructed, two viewings were necessary. "I see dead people," claimed young star Osment in charac-

253

ter. The producers could have said, "We see people lined up at the box office."

The Cider House Rules was directed by Lasse Hallstrom from the novel by John Irving, who also wrote the screenplay. Tobey Maguire starred along with Michael Caine and Charlize Theron. The movie was a subtle pro-choice exercise, rendered with artistry.

The Insider was a movie about the absolute power the tobacco industry wields over the American way of life. Australian Russell Crowe played the tobacco executive who wrestled with his conscience to do the right thing only to be confronted by more powerful forces. Al Pacino and Christopher Plummer were, as always, excellent.

Also Notable: *The Talented Mr. Ripley* starring the talented Matt Damon and *The Matrix*, a brilliantly realized sci-fi flick starring Keanu Reeves. And, last but not least, *Star Wars: Episode I—The Phantom Menace* became the third largest–grossing film of all time.

THE PLAYERS

Angelina Jolie's performance in *Girl, Interrupted* earned her an Oscar, but her performance that night earned her some very bad publicity. Jolie hugged and kissed the man seated next to her and offered her love to him from the stage. Nothng wrong about that, except that the man was her brother. Both were children of actor Jon Voight.

Hilary Swank appeared in *Boys Don't Cry* as a woman of confused sexual identity who dressed as a man. Swank proved she was definitely a beautiful woman as she accepted her Best Actress Oscar.

MUSIC

Ricky Martin had been a member of the Latino boy group Menudo and then a sometime actor, having appeared on the soap "General

Hospital." When he appeared on the Grammy awards, he became an "overnight" sensation. His first English-language CD, simply titled "Ricky Martin," shot off like a rocket. The hit single "Livin' La Vida Loca" was the anthem for the year. Like rock heartthrobs Ricky Nelson and Bobby Sherman before him, his presence may not be lasting, but he significantly changed American music in one way. He was the first Latin to crossover to the mainstream, bringing with him in his wake Enrique Inglesias, Marc Anthony and others. The American sound definitely had a Latin beat from here on.

Teenaged Britney Spears proved that it was a girl's world, too. Her "Baby, One More Time" went to the top of both the album and single charts.

Christina Aguilera released her self-titled album and hit number-one status with the single "Genie in a Bottle."

It was New Jersey–native Lauryn Hill's year at the Grammys. She picked up 5, including Album of the Year and Best New Artist.

Former Beatle George Harrison was nearly killed in his own home by an intruder. Nobody bothers Ringo. Ever.

IN THE NEWS

On February 12, the United States Senate acquitted Bill Clinton on two articles of impeachment that spared him from being the first president ever removed from office. Clinton was only the second president to be impeached, the other being Andrew Johnson during Reconstruction.

On April 20, two high school students, Eric Harris and Justin Klebold went on a killing rampage at Columbine High School in Colorado using guns and homemade bombs. The upscale community, having felt insulated from the terrors of violence, recoiled. Major media attention surrounded Columbine and used it as the benchmark of all teen violence. Was so much attention paid here and not, say, Pearl, Mississippi, because Columbine was an upper-middle-class community?

Elian Gonzalez fled Cuba on a raft with his mother. She didn't survive the trip. The 6-year-old refugee became a pawn in an international game of chess.

The Y2K bug, or virus, was on everyone's mind. Computer technicians apparently knew for some time that there was a potential problem when systems converted from the year 1999 to 2000 but they didn't bother telling anyone. Doomsayers insisted that the moment the clocks hit midnight on the night of December 31, the world's computer systems would cease to operate correctly. Others found comfort in the words of Nostradamus who predicted the end of the world at the second millennium. Still others readied their survival gear for the apocalypse to come. As it happened, nothing happened, except a good time at New Year's Eve parties. Oh, yes, there was a pocket of individuals who insisted that the real turning of the millennium didn't occur until midnight, December 31, 2000 and that's when the disasters would strike.

THIS ACTUALLY HAPPENED (PART V)

He was famous before he knew how to utter his first name. His every move from childhood on was recorded for public consumption. America watched him grow from the young boy who saluted his father's funeral cortege to become the founder and publisher of *George*, a political magazine. As the son of the 35th President and his elegant wife, John F. Kennedy, Jr. held a special place in the hearts of Americans. While some younger people didn't understand what the fuss was all about, John-John, as he was called in the media, carried himself with a rare dignity. He understood his place as a son of great wealth and influence. And while his cousins often found their names splattered in the newspapers for all the wrong reasons, John F. Kennedy, Jr. honored his famous name by doing good works. On July 16, John F. Kennedy, his wife Carolyn Bissette Kennedy and her sister Lauren Bissette were killed in a plane accident off the coast of Cape Cod. They were on their way to his cousin Rory's wedding. John F. Kennedy, Jr.'s death came as a shock to a nation who had remembered the day he was born.

John's uncle Joseph Jr. and his aunt Kathleen died in plane crashes.
Aristotle Onassis's son Alexander died in a plane crash.
Ethel Kennedy's parents and brother died in plane crashes.
Senator Ted Kennedy nearly died in a plane crash.

SPORTS

In Superbowl XXXIII fever, the Denver Broncos did it again, beating the Atlanta Falcons 34–19. Broncos quarterback John Elway won the MVP award after throwing 29 passes, connecting with 18, for a total of 336 yards.

National Hockey League legendary star Wayne Gretzky ended his career on the ice.

American icon, Joe DiMaggio died at the age of 84. Critics aside, the man lived his life in an exemplary fashion. A man with faults, to be sure, he maintained a dignity and aura that many could not understand and often wished to tarnish. He single-handedly gave many Americans of another, earlier generation hope that the American dream can happen to anyone as long as they could hit and field a ball.

TELEVISION

President Clinton offered his side of what happened with Monica Lewinsky in a taped deposition that was aired over and over. His evasions had him utter the immortal phrase, "It depends on what your definition of 'is' is." Such clumsy equivocations wouldn't be uttered by television's fictional President, Jed Barlet, another liberal, but one more adept at handling the media on the hit show "The West Wing." While the Clinton story raged on, Americans tuned into this show that demonstrated a White House under control during difficult times. Wishful thinking, perhaps, for the real-life, troubled executive.

"The Sopranos" debuted on HBO on January 10. James Gandolfini starred as Tony Soprano, a New Jersey gangster with problems with both his "family" and his family. Nancy Marchand played Livia, the biggest mother of them all. The public's itchy fascination with the mob was now scratched on a regular basis.

On August 16, "Who Wants to Be a Millionaire" debuted. It captured large audiences much like the quiz shows of the 1950s. Regis Philbin was the host and even his color-on-color style of dress caught on. The show ushered in what's been called "Reality Television" with such hits as "Survivor" and the game show "The Weakest Link" following in its path.

In 1995, "The Jenny Jones Show" pushed the envelope so far that an actual murder took place in the aftermath of one episode. Gay guest Scott Amedure was murdered by another guest, Jonathon Schmitz, after confessing to Jones on an un-aired episode that he had a gay crush on Schmitz. In 1999, the courts found the show negligent.

In the biggest news of the year for her many fans, soap star Susan Lucci finally took home an Emmy for her work on "All My Children." This, after 18 losses.

FADS AND FASHION

Tattooing and body-piercing become fashion trends. At least the piercing will heal, but years from now how will a businessman explain that skull-and-crossbone tattoo on his forehead?

THE
2000s

After experiencing the longest growth in a non-wartime era, the economy was on the minds of more and more Americans. Large companies had begun to take less and less responsibility for their longtime employees and put more onus on the individual to secure retirement funds. As companies rolled back on pension plans as an employee benefit, those employees were offered 401(k) plans as an option. In many cases, this was their only source of savings. Thus, with more people enrolled in a retirement plan like 401(k), more individuals became directly involved with the stock market. They had to pay attention. Only a generation before, an employee with a corporation didn't think much about investment possibilities since the company had a pension plan in place. Those days were definitely over.

The good news was the economy was booming. The Internet had allowed for hundreds if not thousands of new start-up companies to operate. Risky at best, both investors and employees of these new companies were in for a rocky time ahead.

President Clinton had blown his chance to take America down a more moderate path. His brand of Democratic policies were far more central than the right wing would have Americans believe. He promised and delivered to "end welfare as we know it." His personal idiosyncrasies nearly did him in, and in the minds of many, should have done so. Clinton's reckless personal ways extended to his last days in office when he pardoned a group of people who otherwise were unpardonable.

Hillary Rodham Clinton made history by being the only First Lady to seek and secure elected office as Senator representing New York. Many called her a "carpetbagger" for using New York as a base for her own political goals. She wasn't the first person to do this. In the 1960s, Robert F. Kennedy had become a senator from

New York with very little time spent in that state. There are those in New York City, in particular, where Mrs. Clinton was very popular, who believed that anyone could be a New Yorker since many residents of New York were new transplants.

George W. Bush was a brand-name president, the son of a known commodity who, regardless of his lack of experience, became president more because of his father than because of who he was himself. Whatever his true political nature, he would be hampered by a 50–50 split in the Senate and a small majority in the House. His affable good nature belied the fact that he had surrounded himself with thorough-going professionals, such as Vice President Dick Cheney, General Colin Powell, the first African-American to hold such high political office as Secretary of State, and Donald Rumsfeld, the Secretary of Defense. These men had served his father well, and "Dubbya," as the president was nicknamed for his middle initial, respected loyalty. Unlike John F. Kennedy who spoke of "a torch being handed to a new generation," George W. Bush was resolved to hand it back to an older one.

America had become a Starbucks nation. The Seattle-based firm had taken the phrase "wake up and smell the coffee" literally. They opened up shops all across the country. America needed the caffeine to maintain its hectic pace. Both Mom and Dad worked hard to keep up with the staggering wealth that was cropping up everywhere.

Suburbia had once been the destination of forlorn middle-class urbanites desperate for a better way of life for their children. The recent suburban sprawl was the mandate of hugely successful entrepreneurs who built luxury homes in the middle of what only years before had been cow pastures.

The economic boom helped cities revitalize their decaying centers. Crime was down, with more criminals than ever behind bars. Cities were safer and since manufacturing had long left the urban areas, the service economy grew. People traveled to large cities for exotic food consumption, boutique shopping and a glimpse of diversity.

American cities were the homes of the new immigrants from

places such as India, Pakistan, and Persia (who wanted to mention Iran?). Small towns and rural areas were becoming homogenized by the growth of Wal-Mart and other discount chains. Small, independent concerns could not keep up with the larger stores and their business suffered, leading many to go out of business altogether.

2000

THE MOVIES

Traffic and *Erin Brockovich* were two totally different movies in both content and sensibility. *Traffic* told three interlocking stories of the drug trade in America, without blinking an eye and without handing out a pat Hollywood ending. *Erin Brockovich* was based on a real-life woman who fought to bring about the biggest settlement against a major corporation for its wrongdoing. It was dubbed "a feel-good" crowd-pleaser. Both films were directed by Steven Soderbergh, who had made a name for himself with such films as *Sex, Lies and Videotape*. Soderbergh brought out the best in both casts, but most especially Catherine Zeta-Jones and Michael Douglas.

Gladiator was a big-screen spectacle like *Ben Hur* and *Spartacus* before it. What separated this film from all the others, though, was the up-to-date special effects. Audiences believed they were in decadent Rome. Director Ridley Scott, responsible for such films as *Alien* and *Thelma and Louise,* outdid himself in bringing the story of a great general turned gladiator to the screen.

Also Notable: *Crouching Tiger, Hidden Dragon* directed by Ang Lee. The film made over $100,000,000. Not bad for what essentially was a Kung Fu movie with subtitles.

THE PLAYERS

Russell Crowe got tangled up in the messy divorce of Meg Ryan and Dennis Quaid when he became "the other man," no matter how short-lived his relationship was with Ryan. Tabloids ate it up. Crowe's behavior had always bordered on the anti-social, so it was a great testament to his talent when overcoming all the negative press he had earned, he took home a much-deserved Oscar for *Gladiator.*

Jennifer Lopez showed up at the Academy Awards in another very revealing outfit that had broadcast directors going out of their minds in attempts to cover up the obvious. Lopez's romantic relationship with rap producer Sean "Puffy" Combs had come to a halt after he had been arrested the prior year for gun possession.

The Best Supporting Actress category had become a taking-off point for the children of stars. Mira Sorvino (Paul's daughter) and Angelina Jolie (Jon Voight's kid) had both taken home the prize. Now it appeared a shoe-in for Goldie Hawn's sprout, Kate Hudson, to waltz home with Oscar. Goldie herself had won in the category in 1969. Hudson had been named for her work in *Almost Famous*, Cameron Crowe's follow-up to *Jerry Maguire*. However, the Academy honored a deserving veteran, Marcia Gay Harden, for her work in *Pollock*.

MUSIC

Born Marshall Bruce Mathers III in Kansas City, Missouri, Eminem deservedly gets tagged music's "bad boy." Eminem's album "The Marshall Mathers LP" sold 1.76 million copies in the U. S. in its first week, eventually topping 7 million copies by year's end. It sets a record for a solo artist. What set Eminem apart was his lyrics of hate against blacks, women, and gays. His stance hits a target audience.

Rock and Roll secrets revealed! Rock legend David Crosby was the father of lesbian singer Melissa Etheridge's two children. Both children were the product of artificial insemination, in case they ever wondered how all this happened. Crosby, who received a new liver in 1995, was happy to be giving this time.

IN THE NEWS

Elian Gonzalez was returned to his father in Cuba. Finally.

Senator Joe Lieberman of Connecticut became the first Jewish candidate for national public office when Vice President Al Gore selected him as his running mate.

THIS ACTUALLY HAPPENED (PART VI)

Although it sounds like something out of "Dynasty," the presidential election of 2000 actually happened this way. Former President George Bush had two sons, one the governor of Texas, the other the governor of Florida. The one from Texas was running for president againt Vice President Al Gore. The Texas governor needed to carry Florida to win. The Florida governor promised his brother that would happen. On election night, the major networks declared Florida going to Gore. On national television before the results were in, former President George Bush said that there would be a recount. And recount there was, missing chads, absentee ballots and all. The election of 2000 stretched out into January, 2001. The happy Bush family had another one of its own back in the White House. This hadn't happened in American history since the Adams family. Spooky, huh?

DRUGS

Baseball player Darryl Strawberry and actor Robert Downey, Jr. continued to make news as they battled with their drug addictions.

SPORTS

Not since 1956 had there been a subway series in New York. Then the New York Yankees beat the Brooklyn Dodgers 4 out of 7 games. The Dodgers soon packed up and moved to Los Angeles. This time the Yankees routed the New York Mets in only 5 games. The Yankees were once again, after several World Series wins, legendary.

On June 15–18, Tiger Woods won the U.S. Open. On July 20–23, he won the British Open and on August 17–20, he won the PGA.

TELEVISION

Hollywood bad boy Charlie Sheen's career started to shine when he replaced Michael J. Fox on ABC's "Spin City." Fox had left the hit show to concentrate on his family and his health. He'd been battling Parkinson's disease for some time. Sheen, whose career high points included *Platoon*, was often the star of the tabloids with his bouts with drugs and Hollywood hookers. His image was in stark contrast to the squeaky-clean Fox. But Sheen brought new life to the show and the ratings grew, an unusual event in television when one star is replaced by another. What also made the news so odd was that "Spin City" was aired opposite the NBC hit "The West Wing," which starred Sheen's real-life father, Martin Sheen.

"Survivor," a reality-based show debuted on CBS on May 31, giving a new definition to Memorial Day. The series takes off. The unknown contestants become celebrities in an era when by merely appearing on television you become a celebrity of note. Quick! Name the winner. (Richard Hatch.)

2001

THE MOVIES

Bridget Jones's Diary, based on Brit Helen Fielding's novel of the same name gave Renee Zellweger a chance to turn the tables on our friends across the pond. The very English Vivien Leigh had played two of the most notable American heroines in *Gone with the Wind* and *A Streetcar Named Desire*. Now American Zellweger wore the shoes of the archetypal young British woman, Ms. Jones. She was ably assisted by Colin Firth and the man who every producer turns to when a role calls for a sophisticated Englishman, Hugh Grant.

The late director Stanley Kubrick had long planned *A. I. Artificial Intelligence*, but died before he could get around to making it. The sci-fi dazzler was put into the hands of Steven Spielberg, who, of course, could grab whatever property he wanted. Spielberg's science-fiction credentials were in order, having delivered big-time with *E. T. The Extraterrestrial* and *Close Encounters of the Third Kind*. Still, it would have been interesting to see what Kubrick, the man behind *2001: A Space Odyssey*, would have done in 2001 with this futuristic tale.

THE PLAYERS

Heath Ledger was yet another Australian taking America by storm. He first caught audiences' attention in *Patriot* with Mel Gibson, but came into his own with the hit movie *A Knight's Tale*.

Catherine Zeta-Jones. No relation to Bridget, but her show business connections are impeccable, having married Michael Douglas,
son of Kirk, in one of 2000's most photographed nuptuals. Zeta-
Jones sprang forth in *Zorro,* opposite Antonio Banderas in 1998
and became fully realized as a screen presence in *Traffic.* Zeta-
Jones, a throwback to old Hollywood glamour in the tradition of
Ava Gardner and Rita Hayworth, also established herself as an ac-
tress. In *America's Sweethearts,* she costarred with the true
American sweetheart, Julia Roberts, fresh from her Oscar win for
Erin Brockovich.

Superstar Tom Cruise and his wife Nicole Kidman divorce. It ends
Cruise's second marriage. His first was to Mimi Rogers, a union
that ended in 1990.

THEATER

After years of revival after revival taking center stage on Broadway, it seemed as if the public would be offered only tired rehashes
of things that weren't that good to begin with. Enter that master of
mayhem, Mel Brooks to set American musical comedy on its ear.
His Broadway version of his 1968 film comedy *The Producers* was
a runaway success. Consider the numbers: The day after the show
opened, the box office sold thirty-three thousand five hundred and
ninety-eight tickets, taking in $3,029,197. Nice day's work. Brooks,
in his seventies, had brought real excitement back to the Great
White Way. The story, as insane and insensitive as ever, was hilari-
ous. Everybody laughed, except a Nazi or two.

MUSIC

Bob Dylan turned 60 on May 24. He also took home an Oscar
for the song he did for the film *Wonder Boys.* He was also the subject of several biographies, all trying to figure out the enigma that
was Dylan. The best of the biographies was "Positively Fourth
Street."

Destiny's Child have been called the new Supremes, but they have a hip sound all their own. Their hit album and single, "Survivor," continued at the top of the charts.

George Harrison's doctors announced that the former Beatle and rock legend had battled lung cancer.

Eddie Van Halen, the lead singer of Van Halen, announced that he was also battling cancer.

IN THE NEWS

Oklahoma City bomber Timothy McVeigh was scheduled to be executed on May 16, but documents were found that the FBI had earlier not revealed. His death was to be witnessed via closed circuit television by relatives of his victims and survivors.

President Bush appointed a commission to look into the Social Security System. Yes, it will run out of money within the next few decades and if the president has his way, people will be paying for their own old age, just like the good old days in the Depression.

California millionaire Dennis Tito paid an estimated $20 million to the Russians so that he could be the first "tourist" in space. Not only will Tito go a far distance on that money, but that $20 million will go a long way in helping the Russian economy.

DRUGS

Yes, Darryl Strawberry and Robert Downey, Jr. were still publicly dealing with their demons, but so were others such as "The West Wing" producer/creator Aaron Sorkin. Have talent, achieve great things and then blow it all on drugs. Was this the message that people were hearing over and over?

272 WHAT WAS HOT!

SPORTS

Tiger Woods played the Fantastic Four! In the history of all sports, he achieved an amazing feat. He won the United States Open in the summer of 2000. He won the British Open in July, 2000, the PGA in August, 2000 and topping it off, the Masters on April 5–8, 2001. He was the first to win four consecutive professional majors.

How would you like to be 25 years old, play shortstop for the Texas Rangers and have to live on a paltry $252 million for the next ten years? That's what happened to Alex Rodriguez, giving him by far the richest contract ever awarded an athlete. Put another way, he's worth a quarter of a billion dollars. Play ball!

On February 18, NASCAR legend Dale Earnhart was killed during the last lap of the Daytona 500 when his car slammed into a wall. Frayed seat belts were reported to be possibly at fault.

TELEVISION

As with many A-list Hollywood stars unable to find work in studio-produced features, Sally Field returned to television as a guest star on "ER." Field started her career as "Gidget," and looked upon television at the time as a stepping-off point. Coming full circle, she took what was offered to her. Others found television, and mostly cable outlets, more viable for the their craft, such as director Mike Nichols and Emma Thompson, who collaborated on "Wit."

She won't go away. Marilyn Monroe was unearthed by, among all people, Joyce Carol Oates in her novel *Blonde*. The novel made its way onto the CBS airwaves in May as a miniseries.

"Queer as Folk" debuted on Showtime. This gay soap opera, set in a very fictional Pittsburgh, Pennsylvania, pushed the envelope about as far as it could go, depicting gay sex in astoundingly vivid detail. Was the mainstream ready for this? Stay tuned.

An import from Britain, "The Weakest Link" was another question-and-answer show but one with a twist. Instead of sympathizing with a losing contestant, this show humiliated him or her, sending the person down the "walk of shame." What's next, the "Mao Tse Tung Hour"? Host Anne Robinson became a cult favorite for her straight-laced nastiness.

FADS AND FASHION

E-trading was now being done on the run. Kiosks, much like those omnipresent ATM machines, were popping up everywhere so that investors could make e-trades as they bought their morning coffee.

Not so much fashion as a swan song to good taste, singer Bjork's outrageous outfit at the Academy Awards had critics squawking. Dressed inside a dead swan-like dress, it proved the singer to be a birdbrain when it comes to fashion.

SPORTS

The Williams sisters proved to be the focus of national attention as they vied for the U.S. Open against each other in the finals. While Venus ultimately beat out her sister Serena, the two were both winners in the hearts of Americans, who watched the event in prime-time by the millions.

SEPTEMBER 11, 2001

America under attack. At 8:45 AM (Eastern Daylight Time) a hijacked passenger jet out of Boston crashed into the north tower of New York City's 110-story World Trade Center, tearing a gaping hole into the building and setting it on fire. About 18 minutes later, a second hijacked airliner, also out of Boston, crashed into the south tower of the World Trade Center and exploded. Both towers were set ablaze. At 9:43, an airliner out of Washington, D.C., crashed into the Pentagon; the remainder of the building was evacuated as was the White House. At 10:05, the south tower of the World Trade Center collapsed, plummeting unbelievably to the streets below. At 10:10, a fourth hijacked airliner out of Newark, bound for San Francisco, crashed into rural Somerset County, Pennsylvania, southeast of Pittsburgh. At 10:13, the United Nations in New York was evacuated. In Washington, the State and Justice departments were evacuated. At 10:28 the north tower of the World Trade Center collapsed. Two of the great symbols of American prosperity and liberty were reduced to ashes in lower Manhattan. Buildings across the country were evacuated. At 1:27 PM, a state of emergency was declared by the city of Washington, D.C. At 5:20, the 47-story Building 7 of the World Trade Center collapsed.

Besides those known to be on the doomed airliners, thousands of people in New York and Washington were reported missing, most presumed dead, including hundreds of firefighters, police and rescue workers.

At 8:30 PM, President Bush addressed the nation, saying "thousands of lives were suddenly ended by evil." After asking for prayers for the families and friends of the victims, he declared "These acts shattered steel, but they cannot dent the steel of American resolve."

Americans were bound together by these unspeakable acts and for the first time in many people's memories, talk of war was everywhere. Democrats and Republicans all stood behind the president.

The prime suspect behind these heinous acts was Osama bin Laden, the terrorist leader who was hiding in Afghanistan. As Americans sat riveted to their televisions, watching the terrible destruction pile up and the death toll rise, the focus of the American military operation was finding bin Laden and taking him out.

Internationally, America had the support of nations around the globe. Moments of silence were held in capital cities everywhere on the planet.

This unprecedented attack on America was felt as deeply as the attack on Pearl Harbor, which had inaugurated our participation in World War II. In many ways these attacks were worse. After all Pearl Harbor was a military installation and we knew that we had been attacked by a foreign nation, Japan. September 11, 2001, was different. Civilians were dead, dying, and suffering. America's way of life was under attack. There was no single nation that could be pointed to as the enemy of the United States.

While uncertainty filled the hearts of each American, there was a steely determination to bring justice to the world. In the past, America had been faced with challenges that seemed this insurmountable, but they were overcome. No matter the challenge, America was ready, willing and able. No matter the price, America would pay it. No matter what, America was the land of the free and the home of the brave.

About the Author

Julian Biddle is the pseudonym of a well-published playwright and journalist who resides in New York City and eastern Pennsylvania.